Updated Second Edition

T0384675

Activity Book 6

with Online Resources

British English

Caroline Nixon & Michael Tomlinson

Cambridge University Press
www.cambridge.org/elt

Cambridge Assessment English
www.cambridgeenglish.org

Information on this title: www.cambridge.org/9781316628799

© Cambridge University Press & Assessment 2009, 2015, 2017

First published 2009
Second edition 2015
Updated second edition 2017

20

Printed in Poland by Opolgraf

A catalogue record for this publication is available from the British Library

ISBN 978-1-316-62879-9 Activity Book with Online Resources 6
ISBN 978-1-316-62771-6 Pupil's Book 6
ISBN 978-1-316-62796-9 Teacher's Book 6
ISBN 978-1-316-62901-7 Class Audio CDs 6 (4 CDs)
ISBN 978-1-316-62948-2 Teacher's Resource Book with Online Audio 6
ISBN 978-1-316-62857-7 Language Portfolio 6
ISBN 978-1-316-62982-6 Interactive DVD with Teacher's Booklet 6 (PAL/NTSC)
ISBN 978-1-316-62805-8 Presentation Plus 6
ISBN 978-1-316-62872-0 Posters 6

Additional resources for this publication at www.cambridge.org/kidsbox

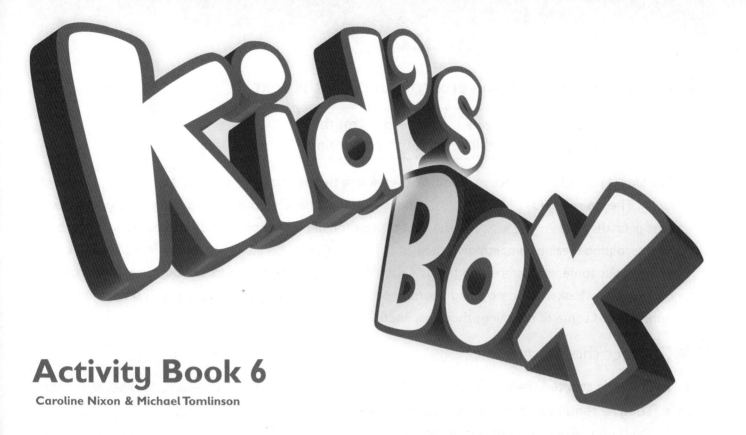

Kid's Box

Activity Book 6

Caroline Nixon & Michael Tomlinson

High technology

1 Choose words from the box to complete the text.

excited	going	~~started~~	thirtieth	maths
won	laughed	horrible	year	something

The kids **(1)** _started_ back at school last week and they're ready for another **(2)** _____ of study. They're really **(3)** _____ about working on *Kid's Box* again, their ezine for young people. Last year they **(4)** _____ the school prize for the best project and this year they want to win an international ezine competition if they can. They're **(5)** _____ to visit lots of places and write about some very interesting things. Last Wednesday they met to talk about their new project and they also looked at some funny photos from last year. They **(6)** _____ a lot when they remembered some of the things that happened.

2 Correct the sentences.

1 The kids started their holidays last week. _The kids started back at school last week._
2 They're ready for another month of study. _____
3 They won the school prize for art. _____
4 They met last Friday. _____
5 They watched some funny DVDs. _____
6 They cried a lot when they remembered. _____

3 Write sentences.

1   **2**   **3**   **4**   **5**   **6**

1 _We use a toothbrush to clean our teeth._   4 _____
2 _____   5 _____
3 _____   6 _____

4 Answer the questions.

1 What did you do during the holidays? _____
2 Where did you go? _____
3 Who did you see? _____
4 What did you eat? _____
5 What did you do? _____
6 Who were you with? _____

5 Put the words in groups.

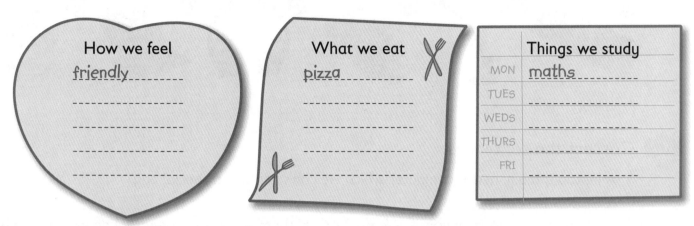

| ~~maths~~ | ~~friendly~~ | ~~pizza~~ | geography | excited | interested | salt | English |
| bored | salad | pleased | sandwich | history | pepper | science | |

How we feel
friendly_____
_____
_____
_____
_____

What we eat
pizza_____
_____
_____
_____
_____

Things we study

MON	maths_____
TUES	_____
WEDS	_____
THURS	_____
FRI	_____

6 Find the letters on the clock. Make words.

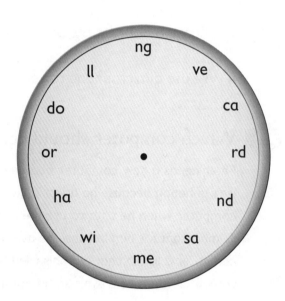

1 It's twenty-five to twelve.   wing_____
2 It's twenty-five past six.   _____
3 It's twenty to eleven.   _____
4 It's ten past one.   _____
5 It's ten to nine.   _____

Clock letters: ng, ve, ll, ca, do, rd, or, nd, ha, sa, wi, me

7 Write times to make four more words.
You can use the same letters again.

1 It's ten to eleven. (doll)_____
2 _____
3 _____
4 _____

8 Find and write the adjectives.

iped
ired
uge
errible
mous
orrible
ong
~~mazing~~
oft
ngerous
rk
t
potted
vely
ud
wake

a_mazing_____
a_____
fa_____
fa_____
da_____
da_____
s_____
s_____

h_____
h_____
lo_____
lo_____
str_____
str_____
t_____
t_____

9 Sort and write the words. Label the pictures.

| ~~bakydroe~~ | nep irved | cawmeb | corphimneo | adephoshen | toppla |

1 **2** **3** **4** **5** **6**

Keyboard _____   _____   _____   _____   _____   _____

10 Correct the sentences.

1 A laptop is a big, heavy computer which we can't carry in a special bag.
A laptop is a small, _____

2 Speakers are like microphones. We use both of them to see our friends when we chat with them.
_____

3 The whiteboard is the part of the computer which has the letters and numbers. We use it to draw
_____

4 We use a microphone to carry information from one computer to another.
_____

11 Which computer should Peter buy? Tick (✓) the correct box.

Peter needs a new computer because the one he has got is very old. It hasn't got a DVD player but he isn't unhappy because he doesn't like watching films on the computer. He has a lot of problems with his old computer when he tries to use the internet because it is too slow and he can't use it with wifi. The internet is important for him because he uses it to search for information for his school projects. He also uses his computer a lot to chat with his friends, but he never uses it to play games. He doesn't need to carry his computer when he travels so he doesn't want a laptop. He thinks it's a good idea to buy a pen drive to take projects and songs round to his friend's house.

The KB4

Speakers
DVD player
Big screen - great for playing games
Special keyboard £425

The KB5
Laptop computer
DVD player
Speakers

Better memory
Good for the internet £350

The KB6
FREE!

DVD player
Webcam
Microphone
Speakers
Good for the internet
Free pen drive £395

DVD player

12 Write three reasons why you chose that computer in your notebook.

13 Join two words to make one. Write the new word.

1 home — ball   ----------------------
2 head   board   ----------------------
3 key   room   ----------------------
4 class   work   <u>homework</u>----------
5 basket   phones ----------------------

14 Write another word at the end to make new words.

1 bath<u>room</u>_____   3 ear_____   5 arm_____   7 foot_____

2 book_____   4 hand_____   6 tooth_____   8 snow_____

15 Find eight differences.

<u>In picture a, the boy's chatting online. In picture b, he's watching a film.</u>

----

16 Answer the questions.

1 Can you use a computer? _____

2 Do you write emails? _____

3 Do you use apps to chat with your friends? _____

4 Have you got wifi at home? _____

5 Do you use a pen drive? _____

6 Do you send messages to your friends? _____

7 How do you listen to music? _____

8 Do you prefer headphones or speakers? _____

17 Match the words to make new words.

1 _d_   play   **a** board   **6** _g_   country   **f** ache

2 _   air   **b** ball   **7** _   business   **g** side

3 _   key   **c** shop   **8** _   head   **h** ball

4 _   foot   **d** ground   **9** _   super   **i** man

5 _   book   **e** port   **10** _   volley   **j** market

18 **10 CD1** Listen, check and say.

Lst wknd ptr wnt 2 hs uncls hs in the cntry. Hs uncl lvs on a frm. Hs a frmr. Ptr hlpd hm wth the anmls. He gt up erly and gt the mlk frm the cws, n the egs frm the chckns. Thrs a smll drty lak on the frm n ptr fll in2 it. lol.

When we use text language:
• We take out the vowels:
  clssrm – classroom
• We use words or letters that sound the same, but are shorter:
  hw r u (= How are you?)
• Some people don't use punctuation or capital letters in a short message.

Write it right

19 Write the text above correctly.

Last weekend

20 Write a text message for your friend to read.

21 Read and answer.

1 What time's Diggory giving his talk?

At half past two.

2 What kind of computer has Diggory got?

3 What can he use to explain ancient maths and technology?

4 Who's Sir Doug Bones?

5 Why does he want to look under the cloth?

6 Who's got the calendar at the end?

22 Look at the code. Write the secret message.

A	B	C	D	E	F	G	H	I	J	K	L	M

N	O	P	Q	R	S	T	U	V	W	X	Y	Z

I h e   _ _ _ _

_ _ _ _ _   _ _ _ _ _ _   _ _ _ _ _ _ _

_ _ _ _   _ _ _ _   _ _ _ _ _ _   _ _ _ _ _ .

? **Do you remember?**

1 10.55 is five to _____ eleven.

2 _____ don't we buy a new computer?

3 I bought a _____ , so now I can see my friends when we talk on the computer.

4 A small computer which we can carry easily is a _____ .

5 _____ and _____ are two new words we can make from 'ball', 'play', 'foot' and 'ground'.

6 In text language 'U' means _____ .

Can do

I can name the parts of a computer.

I can talk about technology.

I can write text messages in English.

1 Beastly tales

We use *going to* to talk about plans.

Affirmative	Negative (n't = not)	Question
I'm (am) going to read.	You **aren't going to** listen to music.	**Is** he **going to** play tennis?
She's (is) going to read.	We **aren't going to** listen to music.	**Are** they **going to** play tennis?
We're (are) going to read.	He **isn't going to** listen to music.	**Am** I **going to** play tennis?

1 Correct the sentences.

1 I're going to be in the play. I'm going to be in the play.
2 She's going be the lion. _____
3 Do you are going to watch The Lion King? _____
4 They isn't going to go to the theatre tomorrow. _____
5 What has he going to do at the weekend? _____
6 She hasn't going to wash her hair today. _____

2 Complete the questions. Match them with the answers.

Who	~~Which~~	Where	When	Why	What

1 Which____ bus are you going to catch?
2 _____ are we going to play football?
3 _____ is he going to call?
4 _____ is she going to wash the car?
5 _____ is he going to read?
6 _____ are they going to do the exam?

a He's going to call his mum. ▢
b They're going to do it tomorrow. ▢
c He's going to read his comic. ▢
d I'm going to catch the number 27. ▣ 1
e In the park. ▢
f Because it's dirty. ▢

3 Look at the code. Write the secret message.

=	H	I	J	K	L	M	N	O	P	Q	R	S	T	U	V	W	X	Y	Z	A	B	C	D	E	F	G
	A	B	C	D	E	F	G	H	I	J	K	L	M	N	O	P	Q	R	S	T	U	V	W	X	Y	Z

A O L   A O L H A Y L   J S B I   P Z   N V P U N   A V   Z O V D   A O L   W S H F

The _____ ____ __ _____ __ ____ ___ ____

V U   A O L   S H Z A   A O B Y Z K H F   H U K   M Y P K H F   V M   Q B U L.

__ ___ ____ _____ ___ _____ __ ____.

4 Find six sentences and write them in your notebook.

He isn't	tickets	to rain	animals.
How many	to get	eat	tomorrow.
Are they going	going	do you	monkey.
They didn't	isn't going	for the	an actor.
Lions	choose him	to be	the play?
It	catch and	parts in	want?

5 What are they going to do?

1 Robert's switching on the TV.
He's going to watch TV.

2 Sue's standing outside the castle and she's holding her camera.

3 The car's very dirty. Mr White is walking towards it with some water.

4 Some people are standing at the bus stop.

5 The boys are walking to the park. They're carrying a football.

6 There's some paper in front of Emma and she's picking up a pen.

6 Think about January next year. Answer the questions.

1 How old are you going to be?
2 What class are you going to be in at school?
3 Which subjects are you going to study?
4 Which clubs are you going to join?
5 What are you going to do after school and on which days?
6 Which books are you going to read?
7 Which films are you going to see?
8 What else are you going to do?

7 Use your answers to write about what you're going to do next year.

In January next year, I'm going to be

8 Find the words. Label the picture.

f	a	i	r	i	e	n
n	e	s	t	o	s	h
a	a	a	u	e	c	o
o	g	g	t	e	a	r
e	l	a	o	h	l	n
f	e	o	u	e	f	
c	l	a	w	u	s	r

1 _ _ _ _ _ _ _ _

2 _ _ _ _ _ _ _ _

3 *eagle* _ _ _ _ _

4 _ _ _ _ _ _ _ _   **5** _ _ _ _ _ _ _ _   **6** _ _ _ _ _ _ _ _

9 Look at the other letters in the wordsearch in Activity 8. Cross out all the vowels which aren't 'i'. Write the other letters. _ _ _ _ _ _ _ _

Which beast is it? _ _ _ _ _ _ _ _

10 Look at the picture and correct the sentences.

1 The dragon's got fur on its body. _The dragon's got scales on its body._ _ _ _ _ _

2 The dragon wants to get the parrot's eggs. _ _ _ _ _ _ _ _

3 The dragon and the eagle have got dangerous hands. _ _ _ _ _ _ _

4 The dragon's got feathers on its wings, but the eagle hasn't. _ _ _ _ _ _

5 The dragon's got two ears on its head. _ _ _ _ _ _ _

6 The eagle's eggs are in a cave. _ _ _ _ _ _ _

11 Look at these beasts. Invent names and describe them.

1

This is a 'Dinolion'.
It's got a dinosaur's _ _ _
_ _ _ _ _ _ _ _
_ _ _ _ _ _ _ _
_ _ _ _ _ _ _ _

2

_ _ _ _ _ _ _ _
_ _ _ _ _ _ _ _
_ _ _ _ _ _ _ _
_ _ _ _ _ _ _ _
_ _ _ _ _ _ _ _

3

_ _ _ _ _ _ _ _
_ _ _ _ _ _ _ _
_ _ _ _ _ _ _ _
_ _ _ _ _ _ _ _
_ _ _ _ _ _ _ _

12 Read and answer 'yes' or 'no'.

The Sphinx existed in Ancient Egyptian and Ancient Greek mythology. In Greek mythology the Sphinx had a lion's body, legs and claws, a snake's tail, eagle's wings and a woman's head. The story says that she sat at the door of the ancient city of Thebes to guard it. To go into the city people had to answer the Sphinx's question. If they got it right, they could go into the city. If they got it wrong, she ate them. The Ancient Greek writer, Sophocles, wrote the question in his work. It was 'Which creature goes on four feet in the morning, two feet in the afternoon and three feet in the evening?' Do you know the answer?

1 The Sphinx was a real animal. <u>no</u>_____
2 She had a bird's wings. _____
3 She had a mammal's tail. _____

4 She stood at the door of Thebes. _____
5 She asked people a question. _____
6 People who didn't know went home. _____

13 Write the words.

1 an ancient story about heroes = <u>myth</u>_____
2 snakes have got these on their bodies
   = _____
3 birds have these on their wings = _____
4 a word for animal or creature = _____
5 a very expensive yellow metal = _____
6 some birds make these in trees = _____
7 the home of a king or queen = _____
8 half woman, half fish = _____

14 Now cross out the first letter of each answer in Activity 13. Read the other letters to answer the Sphinx's question.

n	g	a	m̶	f	m
c	m	s	b	a	n

_ ___

15 What's going to happen?

<u>The boat is going to</u>
<u>break on the rocks.</u> _____   _____   _____

_____   _____   _____
_____   _____   _____

16 Complete the sentences.

| mythical | ~~breathes~~ | maths | Thursday | third |
| then | feathers | think | months | clothes |

1 A dragon <u>breathes</u> fire.

2 I'm going to a party and I want to buy some new _____ to wear.

3 These three children came first, second and _____ in the race.

4 My father's birthday is on _____ .

5 We had dinner and _____ we went to the theatre.

6 The unicorn is a _____ animal.

7 I _____ we should watch a film tonight.

8 Parrots are birds with very colourful _____ .

9 There are twelve _____ in a year.

10 Kate's favourite subject is _____ .

17 [20 CD1] Listen, check and say.

18 Complete the story with 'who', 'where' or 'which'.

Write it right

This is the myth of Icarus, the boy
(1) <u>who</u> flew too near to the Sun
and fell out of the sky. Daedalus,
(2) _____ was Icarus' father, was
a clever artist. Minos, (3) _____
was the King of Crete, asked him to make
a labyrinth (4) _____ was very
difficult to get out of. The labyrinth was
the place (5) _____ a terrible
beast called the Minotaur lived.

Writing longer sentences
Join sentences with **who**, **where** and **which**.

Sophocles was a writer. He wrote the Sphinx's question in his work.
➜ Sophocles, **who** was a writer, wrote the Sphinx's question in his work.

The nests are made of gold. Griffins live in them.
➜ The nests **where** griffins live are made of gold.

A dragon is a beast. It has scales and big claws.
➜ A dragon is a beast **which** has scales and big claws.

19 Now write the rest of the story correctly. Use 'who', 'where' or 'which'.

Theseus, / was the son of the King of Athens, decided to save the children from the horrible beast. Ariadne, / was King Minos' daughter, gave Theseus some string / he used when he went into the labyrinth. Theseus went into the place / the beast lived and killed it. The string / Ariadne gave him helped him to find the way out.

King Minos wasn't pleased. He was very angry with Daedalus because he was the man / gave Ariadne the string.

He sent Daedalus to Crete, a small island / he had to stay with his son, Icarus.

Daedalus made some wings / he used to escape from Crete with his son. Icarus felt very happy and flew too near the Sun, / burnt his wings and feathers. He disappeared into the sea below. The place / Icarus fell into the sea is now an island / is called Icaria.

Theseus, who was the son of the King of Athens, decided to save
the children from the horrible beast.

20 Read and answer.

1 Where's the Aztec calendar from? A museum in Mexico City.

2 Who's Iyam Greedy? _____

3 How do you write 6 in the Mayan maths system? _____

4 Who was Quetzalcoatl? _____

5 What's in the email? _____

6 Where are Diggory and Emily going to go? _____

21 Complete and match.

1 How am I going to tell the museum in Mexico City? **d**

2 A spot means one and a _____ means five.

3 It _____ like a phone number to me.

4 I'm a snake and I've got _____ .

5 He was part _____ and part snake.

? Do you remember?

1 They aren't going _____ to choose Dan for the part of the monkey.

2 They are going _____ write about exciting beasts.

3 Dragons have got _____ on their bodies.

4 Eagles live in _____ in high places.

5 _____ is the day before Friday and the day after Wednesday.

6 The place _____ Icarus fell into the sea is now an island called Icaria.

Can do

I can talk about what is going to happen.

I can talk about beasts from myths and legends.

I can write a myth.

1 **Choose words from the box to complete the text.**

| lot | ~~were~~ | There | which | whose |
| was | so | who | many | |

Greek myths **(1)** <u>were</u> full of gods and beasts. The 12 most important gods lived on the Mountain of Olympus. Each god was important for a different area of life. Zeus was very important because he was the King of the gods and was also the father of **(2)** _____ other gods and heroes. Other important gods were Aphrodite (the god of Love), Hades (the god of the Underworld), Athena (the god of the Arts), Apollo (the god of Music) and Poseidon (the Sea god). There were also a **(3)** _____ of different beasts in Greek myths. Some of the famous beasts are the Gorgon, a terrible monster who had snakes on her head; the Chimera, who had three heads; Hydra, **(4)** _____ head grew again if someone cut it off; Pegasus, a horse which had wings; and Cerberus, a huge dog with three heads. There were also frightening dragons and sea snakes **(5)** _____ Greek heroes had a lot of things to worry about!

2 **Read again and answer.**

1 Who was the most important Greek god? <u>Zeus</u> _____

2 Who was Aphrodite? _____

3 Who was the god of Music? _____

4 What was special about the Gorgon? _____

5 Which beast could fly? _____

6 What's the name of the huge dog with three heads? _____

3 **Write about a legend from your country.**

1 What's the name of the hero / heroes? _____

2 What did he / she do? _____

3 Who did he / she do it with? _____

4 Why is he / she famous? _____

A famous legend from my country is _____

Listen and colour and write. There is one example.

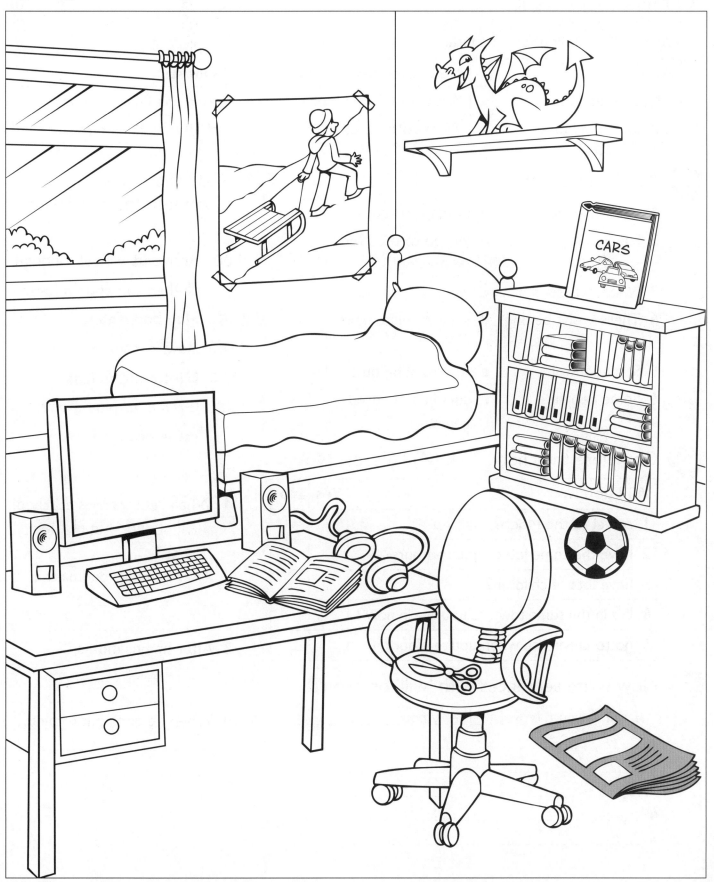

2 Tomorrow's world

LOOK again | Will

We use *will* to talk about the future.

Affirmative	Negative (won't = will not)	Question
I'll go to the Moon.	You won't travel by car.	Will she fly in a rocket?
It'll go to the Moon.	We won't travel by car.	Will they fly in a rocket?

1 Read and match.

1 We will have   **a** invent a carplane. ☐

2 She won't go   **b** will go to the Moon on holiday. ☐

3 NASA will send a   **c** wifi everywhere. [1]

4 There won't be any   **d** solar satellite next year. ☐

5 Someone will   **e** to school by bus. ☐

6 Some people   **f** cars in a hundred years. ☐

2 Complete the chart. Tick (✓) 'Yes' or 'No'.

Will you ...	Yes	No
1 travel to the Moon?		
2 have the same job as your parents?		
3 have lots of children?		
4 live in the same town as you live in now?		
5 go to university when you're older?		

3 Now write sentences with 'will' or 'won't'.

I will / won't travel to the Moon.

1 _____

2 _____

3 _____

4 _____

5 _____

4 Read the notes.
Complete the sentences.

9.00   Arrive at school. Change clothes for sports lesson.

9.15   Play badminton.

10.00 Have a shower.

10.30 Go to maths lesson.

11.15 Go out to play. Drink some orange juice.

1 When Peter arrives at school, he'll change his clothes for sport.

2 After he plays badminton, _____ .

3 After he has maths, _____ .

4 When he goes out to play, _____ .

5 Will these things happen in 2050? Write sentences with 'will' or 'won't'.

1 Children / classes / home <u>Children won't have classes at home.</u>
2 People / go / Mars _____
3 People / fly / cars _____
4 People / use computers _____
5 Children / have electronic course books _____
6 People / use more plastic _____

6 Read and complete.

| quickly | ~~shower~~ | won't | arms | cup | will | clean |

This is my new invention to help children in the future. It's a cross between a **(1)** shower and a car-wash. It'll have two funny metal **(2)** _____ with big gloves made of rubber. These **(3)** _____ move round and round very **(4)** _____ to wash us with soap and water. One of them will **(5)** _____ our teeth with a toothbrush too. Outside the shower there'll be a machine to dry us. It'll look like a big **(6)** _____ which we'll stand under. We'll have a shower and we **(7)** _____ have a wet towel.

7 Design and draw an invention to help children in the future.

8 Write about your invention.

9 Label the photos.

engineer   astronaut   ~~tourist~~   businessman

tourist _____ _____ _____ _____

10 Sort and write the words.

1 Earth_____
2 _____
3 _____
4 _____
5 _____

11 Complete the sentences.

1 Space_____ is the name we give to everything outside Earth's air.
2 An _____ is a person who designs or makes machines or electrical things.
3 We breathe _____ .
4 The planet _____ is where we live.
5 An _____ can travel in space.
6 The _____ goes round our planet. We can see it at night.
7 A _____ visits another town or country on holiday.
8 A man who works in business is called a _____ .
9 A _____ goes very quickly and can take people into space.

12 Read and answer 'yes' or 'no'.

The Space Race started in 1957 when the Soviet Union sent a satellite into space. It was called Sputnik 1. A satellite is something which goes round Earth. The Soviet Union then sent a dog called Laika into space in Sputnik 2. Next, the USA sent its own satellite, called Explorer 1, into space. In 1958 the USA started their space agency called NASA. Three years later in 1961 the Russian, Yuri Gagarin, became the first person to orbit Earth in a spaceship. It wasn't until July 1969 that the American astronaut, Neil Armstrong, became the first person to walk on the Moon.

1 The Soviet Union sent the first satellite into space. yes___
2 The first animal in space was a monkey. _____
3 The USA started NASA in 1959. _____
4 Yuri Gagarin was an astronaut from the USA. _____
5 Gagarin flew round Earth. _____
6 Neil Armstrong was the first man to walk on the Moon. _____

13 Match the ideas about life on Zeron, the space city. Write sentences.

1 telescopes in the windows   **a** to build new houses
2 satellites   **b** to get energy
3 solar panels   **c** to travel into space
4 robots   **d** to look at the stars
5 rockets   **e** to receive signals from space

1

1 <u>We'll have telescopes in the windows to look at the stars.</u>
2 _____
3 _____
4 _____
5 _____

14 Read and answer the riddles.

1 The beginning of Earth, the end of space. The beginning of every end, the end of every place. What am I? 'e' _____

2 What comes once in a minute, twice in a moment and never in a thousand years?

   _____

3 Which letter will come next in this sequence? M, A, M, J, J, A, S, O ... ? _____

4 How will you use the letters in NEW DOOR to make one word? _____

5 Harry was an engineer. His mother had four children. The first was April, the second was May and the third was June. What was the name of her fourth child? _____

6 A man's looking at a photo of a famous astronaut and he says, 'I have no brothers and sisters, but that man's father is my father's son.' Who's he looking at? _____

15 Read and complete the circle with names and jobs.

There are three girls and two boys. They're talking about the jobs they think they will (✓) and won't (✗) do in the future.

1 Sarah's sitting between Dave and Mike. The person on Mike's left thinks she'll be an actress but she won't be a painter.

2 The boy who says he'll be a dentist won't be an actor.

3 The person on Mary's left won't be a photographer but she thinks she'll be a mechanic.

4 The girl next to Lucy loves cameras so she'll be a photographer, but she won't be a cook.

5 The boy next to Lucy loves rockets but he won't be an astronaut. He thinks he'll be a rocket engineer.

16 Match the rhyming words.

1	c	I'll	**a**	feel	**6**	g	I'm	**f**	rule
2	_	she'll	**b**	knees	**7**	_	who's	**g**	time
3	_	they're	**c**	smile	**8**	_	who'll	**h**	don't
4	_	we're	**d**	near	**9**	_	won't	**i**	choose
5	_	he's	**e**	air	**10**	_	let's	**j**	gets

17 [34 CD1] Listen, check and say.

18 Read the Tourist Space Programme and answer.

Holidays in Space

Friday 17 July 2047

7.00 Meet at the Earth Space Station, Houston, Texas, USA.

8.00 Leave Earth in a spaceplane.

8.30 Stop at The Milky Way star café for breakfast (hot chocolate and cake pills).

9.30 Put on spacesuits. Get on the KB6 Adventurer space rocket.

12.00 Arrive on the Moon. Walk around and take photos.

12.30 Go to The Armstrong Moon restaurant for lunch (chicken salad in an envelope). Take off spacesuits to eat.

1.30 Catch a Moon bus to go to the space port.

2.00 Get on the KB6 Adventurer again. Fly to The Galactica Hotel.

1 How will they leave Earth?
In a spaceplane.

2 Where will they stop for breakfast?

3 What will they have for breakfast?

4 What will they put on?

5 What will they do on the Moon before lunch?

6 Why will they take off their spacesuits?

Connectors
• Remember to use some of these words to join your sentences and sequence them:
When, Then, After that, because, before

Write it right

19 Practise saying your answers with the "ll" form correctly.

20 Use your answers to write the Space Programme in your notebook.

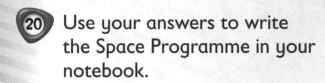

The tourists will meet at the Earth Space Station at seven o'clock. Then they'll leave Earth in a spaceplane at eight o'clock. Before they get on the KB6 Adventurer space rocket, they'll stop

21 Read and answer.

1 Why did Iyam Greedy send them tickets to Mexico City?
<u>There are legends about Aztec gold.</u>

2 What did the Aztecs and the Mayas use to measure time? _____

3 When did the Aztec new year start? _____

4 What will be the longest day of the year? _____

5 What's the date now in the story? _____

6 Will they stay in Mexico City tonight? _____

22 Read and order the text. Write the story in your notebook.

technology and their ancient maths system. Iyam Greedy, who's a pirate and ☐

notebook and talked about a group of stars. There was a man sitting next to them. He ☐

phone number for Diggory in a letter. When Diggory phoned the number, Iyam ☐

only wants to get the Aztec gold and be rich, stole the Sun Stone and left a ☐

Diggory Bones is an archaeologist who teaches at City University. He had the [1]

On the plane to Mexico City, Diggory and his daughter, Emily, looked at a ☐

man from the plane got into a car with Iyam Greedy and followed their bus. ☐

listened to them talking. When Diggory and Emily caught a bus to Teotihuacan, the ☐

talked about Aztec mythology. Then he sent him two plane tickets in an email. ☐

Sun Stone. This is the name for the Aztec calendar, which he had to talk about Mayan (and Aztec) ☐

? **Do you remember?**

1 In the future there <u>will</u>_____ be spaceplanes.

2 That's not a very good paper plane. It _____ fly very far.

3 _____ are people who fly in space in their job.

4 Our planet is called _____ .

5 In the question 'When'll they arrive?', ''ll' is a contraction of _____ .

6 _____ they build a spaceplane for tourists, we'll fly round Earth on our holiday.

Can do   I can talk about what will happen.
I can talk about travel in the future.
I can write about space travel.

1 Write the planets in order (1 = closest to the Sun).

| Saturn | Earth | Neptune | ~~Mercury~~ | Jupiter | Venus | Uranus | Mars |

1 Mercury ....   **2** ....   **3** ....   **4** ....

5 ....   **6** ....   **7** ....   **8** ....

2 Read and complete the factfile.

Mars is the fourth planet from the Sun and is often called the Red Planet. Mars takes 687 days to go round the Sun, so on Mars a year is 687 days long.

Mars has two moons. It also has the biggest volcanic mountain in the solar system. This is called Olympus Mons. It is 27 km high and it has a diameter of 600 km. There are no rivers or lakes on Mars so scientists think there is no life there, but they think it's possible that there's water under the ground.

FACTFILE – PLANETS

Planet: Mars ....

Position from the Sun: ....

Other name: ....

Orbits the Sun every: ....

How many moons: ....

Interesting facts: ....

....

....

....

....

....

....

....

3 Write about Neptune in your notebook.

FACTFILE – PLANETS

Planet: Neptune

Position from the Sun: eighth

Other name: Big Blue Planet

Orbits the Sun every: 165 years

How many moons: eight

Interesting facts: • strongest winds (2,000 km/h)

• has five rings

• coldest planet

Neptune is the eighth planet from the Sun.

4 **Look and read. Choose the correct words and write them on the lines. There is one example.**

rockets   a monkey   a theatre   stars

> You use this to take photos. It isn't a mobile phone.   <u>a camera</u>

~~a camera~~   1 A big road where people can drive fast.   _____   a lion

2 Astronauts use these to fly into space.   _____

3 This is a person who flies a plane.   _____

a mouse   4 This day comes after Wednesday.   _____   an island

5 This animal is a very big cat. It's called 'The King of the Beasts'.   _____

6 This is a piece of land in the sea. There's water all around it.   _____

planets   a driver

7 This is the place where you go to see a play.   _____

8 There are a lot of these in the sky. You can see them clearly at night.   _____

gold   9 There are eight of these in our solar system.   _____   a stadium

10 This yellow metal is very expensive. People make rings and bracelets from it.   _____

a pilot   Thursday   trees   a motorway

Review Units ⭐1 and ⭐2

① **Read the story. Choose a word from the box. Write the correct word next to numbers 1–5.**

tomorrow	engineer	food	will	future	museum	~~favourite~~	drive
rocket	picture						

Friendly

Friendly is the kids' <u>favourite</u> TV programme. It's a comedy and it's very funny. It's about five friends who all live and study in the same school. Last week the friends had an interview with a special teacher to talk about their **(1)** _____ jobs. They had to think about which school subjects they were good at, and where they wanted to work.

Sue wants to study art at university. Jim loves sport and keeping fit and wants to be a fire fighter. Peter loves **(2)** _____ and he says he'll be a cook. Sally says she'll be a taxi driver. Jenny's good at English and drama and wants to be an actor. She says that when she's famous, Sally **(3)** _____ drive her to the film studio, Peter will cook her lovely meals and Sue will paint her a **(4)** _____ and put it in a big, important **(5)** _____ . When Jim asks what he'll do for her, Jenny says her house will never catch fire so he'll have to change his job!

② **Now choose the best name for the story.**

Tick one box.   Past and present ☐   After-school club ☐   Future plans ☐

③ **Read and match the jokes.**

1 What's green and smells like paint?
2 How does a monster count to 13?
3 Which side of an eagle has the most feathers?
4 What do you get if you cross a blue cat with a red parrot?
5 How many seconds are there in a year?
6 Which animal can jump higher than a house?
7 Where can you find a sea without water?
8 Why don't mother kangaroos like rainy days?
9 What goes through towns and up and over hills, but doesn't move?
10 What do you get if you cross a parrot with a tiger?

a The outside.
b All of them can. A house can't jump.
c A purple carrot!
d I don't know, but when it talks you should listen carefully!
e Green paint.
f On its fingers!
g A road.
h On a map!
i Twelve: January the second, February the second …
j Because their children have to play inside!

☐
☐
☐
☐
1
☐
☐
☐
☐
☐

4 Complete the sentences. Count and write the letters.

1 <u>Space</u> is the place outside Earth's air, where the Moon and planets are. **[5]**

2 A griffin's nest is made of _____ . **[ ]**

3 In text language, 'tchnlgy' means _____ . **[ ]**

4 We breathe _____ . It's called 'wind' when it moves over Earth. **[ ]**

5 Somebody who works in space is an _____ . **[ ]**

6 Eagles have got lots of _____ on their wings. **[ ]**

7 A small, light computer that we can carry easily is a _____ . **[ ]**

8 'What _____ you do?' 'I'll ask Michael to help me.' **[ ]**

9 The Sun is the only _____ in our solar system. **[ ]**

10 The _____ is the part of the computer which has the letters which we use to write. **[ ]**

11 A space station uses a _____ to send astronauts into space. **[ ]**

12 An _____ designs cars and motorbikes. **[ ]**

13 We use a _____ to see our friends when we're chatting on the internet. **[ ]**

14 _____ are at the end of a dragon's leg. **[ ]**

5 Write the words in the crossword. Write the message.

(crossword grid with numbered clues 1, 6, 9, 7, 8, 10, 3, 4, 5, 2 and letters s, p, a, c, e filling the vertical 10)

1	2	3	4		5	6		7	8	9	10
											s

!

6 Quiz time!

1 What toy animal did Dan have in the audition? <u>He had</u> _____

2 What was the name of Jason's boat? _____

3 Who fought the Minotaur? _____

4 How will tourists fly into space in the future? _____

5 Which planet is 'the Red Planet'? _____

6 How many moons has Saturn got? _____

7 Write questions for your quiz in your notebook.

3 The great outdoors

LOOK again | Past continuous

We use the *past continuous* to describe what was happening in the past.

Affirmative	Negative	Question
I **was climbing** when I fell.	I **wasn't walking**.	**Was** I **playing**?
You **were climbing** when you fell.	He **wasn't walking**.	**Was** she **playing**?
He **was climbing** when he fell.	They **weren't walking**.	**Were** we **playing**?

1 Read and match.

1 She was skating
2 We were cooking sausages
3 You were flying your kite
4 He was skiing down the hill fast   **when**
5 I was sleeping
6 They were waiting at the station

a he saw a tree in front of him. ☐
b it flew into a tree. ☐
c she fell down. ☐ 1
d the kitchen caught fire. ☐
e their train arrived. ☐
f you phoned me. ☐

2 Look at the pictures. Answer the questions.

1 Was Betty playing volleyball at quarter past eleven? _Yes, she was._
2 Were Frank and Betty doing their homework at quarter past five? _____
3 Was Frank playing the guitar at ten past seven? _____
4 Were Frank and Betty having lunch at twenty-five past one? _____
5 Was Betty cleaning her teeth at half past eight? _____
6 Were Frank and Betty watching TV at ten to five? _____

3 Write four more questions about Frank and Betty in your notebook.

4 Correct two mistakes in each sentence.

1 Richard was ~~run~~ for the bus when he ~~dropping~~ his bag. _running, dropped_
2 Peter and Fred was playing baseball when it start to rain. _____
3 I were putting the food on the table when the man phone. _____
4 Vicky was sail in the sea when she hitted a rock. _____

28

5 Match the sentences with the pictures.

1 We looked at our map. We had to walk through a forest to get to the campsite.

2 In this picture we were eating the sandwiches which John and David got from the café. We couldn't eat the sausages because they burned black!

3 Last week I went camping with my friends John and David. When we got off the bus, it was raining.

4 Our feet were hurting after the long walk and we were tired and hungry when we arrived.

5 It was getting late when we were walking through the forest and it was very dark.

6 This is a picture of me when I was cooking the sausages. I'm not a very good cook.

6 Read and answer 'yes' or 'no'.

1 He went camping with his friends David and John. _yes_

2 It was raining when they got off the bus. _____

3 They had to walk up a hill to get to the campsite. _____

4 The Sun was coming up when they were walking through the forest. _____

5 Their feet were hurting when they arrived at the campsite. _____

6 When he was cooking the sausages, he burned them. _____

7 Read and answer.

Hi Sarah,
This is a funny photo of me at the airport! We were waiting for our plane when I started to feel hungry so I decided to buy an ice cream. There weren't many people waiting to buy one. When I was giving the man the money, someone put their suitcase down on the floor behind me. I didn't see it! I was starting to eat my ice cream when my mum called me to go and catch my plane. I turned quickly and I fell over the suitcase and ... my face went into my ice cream! When I stood up, I had a chocolate ice cream on my nose! My mum thought I looked really funny, so she took the photo!
How were your holidays?
See you soon,
Katy

1 What were Katy and her mum doing in the airport? _They were waiting for the plane._

2 Were there many people waiting to buy an ice cream? _____

3 When did someone put their suitcase down behind her? _____

4 What was she starting to do when her mum called her? _____

5 What did her mum think when she stood up? _____

29

8 Look at the picture. Find the words a–l in the wordsearch.

s	o	o	p	d	r	o	h	r	y
l	e	r	f	n	c	w	e	s	t
e	b	c	e	o	n	t	k	t	g
e	a	h	e	s	r	n	o	s	h
p	c	s	n	k	t	e	n	t	i
i	t	a	t	a	z	y	s	a	l
n	o	e	m	p	n	r	e	t	l
g	r	e	x	p	l	o	r	e	r
b	c	s	q	i	u	g	r	l	a
a	h	t	n	x	s	o	u	t	h
g	r	u	c	k	s	a	c	k	h

9 Write the words. Add the correct letters from Activity 8.

1 _camp_____ = to live and sleep outdoors ⟶ **a**

2 _____ = a bag you can sleep in ⟶ ☐

3 _____ = the opposite of north ⟶ ☐

4 _____ = something you can use to see when it's dark ⟶ ☐

5 _____ = a high place that's lower than a mountain ⟶ ☐

6 _____ = a place where you can sleep ⟶ ☐

10 Write definitions for three more words in Activity 8. Add the correct letters.

-- ☐

-- ☐

-- ☐

11 Look at the code. Write the secret message in your notebook.

N = north   S = south   E = east   W = west

When – 5E – 4N – 2W – 3S – 2W – 1N – 3E – 2S – 4N – 2W – 3S – 2W – 2N – 5E – 1S – 2W – 2S – 2W – 1E – 2N – 2W – 2N – 1E – 1S – 2E – 1W – 2E – 2S – 1E.

a	warm,	carry	walking	always	are
You	dry	and	jacket	a	should
fruit,	hills,	some	a	you	take
rucksack.	the	a	in	mobile	phone. →
→ When	of	water,	bottle	should	you

12 Read the sentences. Draw and write on the map.

 The New Forest is 5 km north of Starton.

 The hills are 3 km east of the New Forest.

 There's a bridge over the river 5 km west of the New Forest.

 2 km south of the hills there's a hotel. Its name is the Happy Inn.

 There's a lake 5 km west of Starton. It's called Windymere.

Old Hampton is 2 km north of Windymere.

 The campsite is 3 km east of Old Hampton.

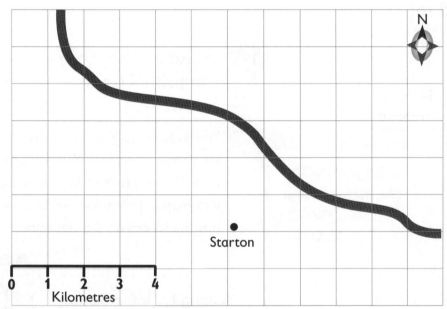

Starton

0 1 2 3 4
Kilometres

13 Now draw these things on the map in Activity 12. Write the directions.

The torch is _____.

The rucksack is _____.

The umbrella is _____.

The suitcase is _____.

14 Find the letters on the clock. Write the words.

1 It's quarter to eight. _south_

2 It's five past ten. _____

3 It's twenty-five past eight. _____

4 It's quarter past six. _____

5 It's twenty past ten. _____

15 Write times to make four more words in your notebook.

16 Circle the correct word.

1 It's cold. I need to put on my **coat** / **goat**.

2 The explorers found a **cave** / **gave** in the mountains.

3 Put your hat and coat in the **call** / **hall**.

4 Kate and John **came** / **game** to the football match.

5 Our teacher said the plate was made of **class** / **glass**.

6 The actor let me **hold** / **gold** the prize he won.

7 He was swimming at the beach when it **got** / **hot** windy.

8 She won a **cold** / **gold** medal at the Olympic Games.

17 Listen, check and say.

18 Read and complete.

| a weekend | Friday | 14 June |
| family | tent for five | ~~website~~ |

12 Greenfield Close
Kidsbridge
KB6 2BU
20 March

Sunnyday Campsite
Cornfield Lane
Hillside

Dear Sir or Madam,
I saw your (1) <u>website</u> on the internet and I'm writing to get some information about your campsite.

I'd like to come with my (2) _____ and we'd like to stay for (3) _____ , from (4) _____ 12 June to Sunday (5) _____ . Please could you tell me if you have a space for these dates?

We haven't got a tent, so I would also like more information about hiring a (6) _____ . Please could you tell me how much this will cost?

On your website it says there's a swimming pool near the campsite. Please could you send me a timetable?

Yours faithfully,

Michael Wishful

19 Write a letter to the campsite. Use the information below.

You want to go with your seven friends for a week in August. You want to go from Tuesday to Monday. You'd like information about horse-riding. There's a riding school on the campsite.

Asking for information
• I'm writing to get some information about ...
• I would like to know ...
• Please could you tell me if / when / what / how ... ?
• Please could you give / send me ... ?

Write it right

Dear Sir or Madam,
I saw your _____
_____
_____
_____
_____
_____
_____
_____
_____

20 Read and answer.

1 Who was getting out of the car behind them? Richard Tricker

2 Where's the Temple of Quetzalcoatl? _____

3 How far is Mexico City from the hotel? _____

4 Why does the man know about this place? _____

5 What does the long street join? _____

6 Was Diggory expecting to see Iyam there? _____

21 Put the verbs into the past.

The story of Mexico City

In about 1325 some young Aztec men **(1)** were getting _____ (are getting) food for their people when

they **(2)** _____ (see) an eagle. It **(3)** _____ (is sitting) on a plant which

(4) _____ (is growing) on a rock in the middle of a lake called Texcoco. They

(5) _____ (think) it **(6)** _____ (is) a special sign and they

(7) _____ (decide) to build their city there.

The Aztecs **(8)** _____ (are) great engineers. They **(9)** _____ (take)

the water away from the lake to make the island bigger. They **(10)** _____ (build) canals

so people **(11)** _____ (can) move around the city by boat, and bridges which they

(12) _____ (take) away at night to protect their city. They **(13)** _____

(call) their city Tenochtitlan and it **(14)** _____ (becomes) one of the biggest and most

important cities in the world at that time. The Aztecs **(15)** _____ (are) very rich because

they **(16)** _____ (have) land, farms, markets and shops. They **(17)** _____

(use) the Mayan number system and calendar and they **(18)** _____ (study) the stars and the

night sky carefully. Like the Ancient Egyptians, they **(19)** _____ (write) with pictures on

a kind of paper. The name of the Aztec people at the time **(20)** _____ (is) 'the Mexica'.

? Do you remember?

1 What were _____ you doing at six o'clock yesterday?

2 I was _____ TV.

3 When I go camping, I sleep in a _____ in my tent.

4 Marco Polo travelled _____ from China to Italy.

5 The teacher told the _____ to do their homework.

6 Please _____ you send me a timetable?

Can do   I can use the past continuous tense to talk about the past.

I can talk about the countryside and follow directions.

I can write a letter asking for information.

33

1 Read and choose the right words.

1 In ancient paintings, the
countryside wasn't …   **a** colourful.   **b** there.   **c** important.

2 Landscape painting became
popular in the …   **a** 5th century.   **b** 18th century.   **c** 20th century.

3 Artists were trying to copy …   **a** nature.   **b** other artists. **c** exams.

4 The French impressionists
started in the …   **a** 1850s.   **b** 1860s.   **c** 1870s.

5 The impressionists used …   **a** big brush strokes. **b** thick lines.   **c** small spots.

6 Gauguin and Van Gogh used …   **a** black and white. **b** bright colours. **c** dark colours.

2 Read and draw a picture. Then compare with your friend.

This picture is a landscape on a sunny day. The top quarter of the picture is the sky which has a big bright sun in the top left-hand corner. On the other side of the page there are three high mountains which have a little snow on top.

There is a stream which comes down from the mountain in the middle and ends in a lake in the bottom right-hand corner of the picture.

There are five tents in a campsite which is to the right of the stream. The tents are all different colours and sizes.

On the left of the picture we can see a small hotel. There are some gardens round the hotel and on one side of the hotel there's a car park. There are two cars in the car park.

3 Write about one of the pictures from Pupil's Book page 35 in your notebook.

This picture is a landscape on

Listen and write. There is one example.

The holiday camp

	Name of camp:	The Lake Camp
1	Price:	.... pounds a night
2	When:	.... to 10th of October
3	Name of lake:	....
4	Take:	....
5	Camp phone number:	....

4 Food, glorious food!

LOOK again — Countable and uncountable nouns

Countable nouns	Uncountable nouns
We can count them: strawberries, olives …	We can't count them: water, bread …
There **aren't enough** chairs.	There **isn't enough** water.
There **are too many** people.	There**'s too much** bread.

1 Follow the uncountable food words.

How much? →

breakfast	water melon	strawberry	chips	egg	fries	lunch	lime
orange	burger	fruit juice	chocolate	lemonade	soup	lemon	orange juice
bread	carrot	flour	sandwich	mango	pasta	sausage	water
rice	milk	meat	coconut	grape	tea	pea	pepper
vegetable	picnic	olives	dinner	beans	coffee	sugar	salt

→ Only a little

2 Read and match.

1 In some countries there isn't	**a** because she felt ill.		
2 They couldn't make any bread	**b** enough food for everyone to eat.	1	
3 He didn't have many eggs	**c** because they didn't have enough flour.		
4 We didn't feel well	**d** so they decided to give some to their friends.		
5 They had too many strawberries	**e** so he bought some more at the supermarket.		
6 She didn't eat much at lunchtime	**f** because we ate too much ice cream at the party.		

3 Read and choose the right words.

1 I feel ill because I ate **too many** / (**too much**) chocolate this morning.
2 I can't buy that because I haven't got **enough** / **too many** money.
3 Are there **too many** / **too much** sandwiches?
4 There aren't **enough** / **too much** buses in my town.
5 I like going to the beach when there aren't **too much** / **too many** people.
6 There isn't **enough** / **too much** juice for everyone.

4 Write four sentences in your notebook about your city.

There are too many cars.
There aren't enough parks.

5 Complete the sentences.

| too many | ~~enough~~ | is |
| too much | haven't | enough |

1 There aren't _enough_ sandwiches for us.
2 There are _____ people on this bus.
3 Have you got _____ time to help me with the cake, Peter?
4 Oh no! I _____ got enough money!
5 There _____ enough milk for everyone.
6 I think we've got _____ homework this weekend.

6 Complete the conversation. Write a letter (A–F) for each answer.

A OK. We won't have sausages. I know. Let's have some rice and chicken.
B Let me see … No, I'm sorry. We haven't got enough spaghetti.
C That's a good idea. So it's chicken, rice and a salad.
D Yes, we all like pizza, but there isn't enough flour or enough cheese.
E ~~I don't know. What would you like?~~
F How about some sausages and a salad?

1 What are we going to have for lunch, Dad? **E**
2 Can we have spaghetti, please? It's my favourite. ☐
3 What about pizza then? Can you make us a pizza, please? ☐
☐
4 OK Dad, what ideas have you got?
5 Er, no thanks. I've had too many sausages this week. I had some on Monday and yesterday. ☐
6 That sounds better. Can we have a salad too, please?
Great. Let's start cooking. ☐

7 Write about the picture. Use 'too much', 'too many', 'enough' and the words in the box.

| ~~chair~~ | fork | water | pasta |
| cake | banana | plate | |

There are enough chairs.
_____
_____
_____
_____
_____
_____

8 What do you think? Answer the questions.

1 Do you eat enough fruit?
_____
2 Do you eat enough fish?
_____
3 Do you eat too much sugar?
_____
4 Do you eat too many sweets?
_____
5 Do you eat too many chips?
_____
6 Do you drink enough water?
_____

9 Label the photos.

| butter | biscuit | chopsticks | jam | ~~snack~~ | pan | sauce | popcorn |

1 snack _____

2 _____

3 _____

4 _____

5 _____

6 _____

7 _____

8 _____

10 Write the words.

1 We put this on food to make it taste better. It can be hot or cold. sauce _____

2 This is something we eat between meals. _____

3 These pieces of wood or plastic are used for eating. _____

4 This is made from fruit. We can put it on bread. _____

5 We use this to cook in. _____

6 Lots of children like these snacks. They are often round. _____

7 This snack is popular when people go to the cinema. _____

8 You can put this on the bread first when you make sandwiches. _____

11 Write definitions for these words.

1 sandwich _____

_____

2 strawberry _____

_____

3 knife _____

_____

12 Read and complete the sentences with 1, 2, 3 or 4 words.

Potato crisps are very popular as a snack all over the world. George Crum invented them in the USA. At the restaurant where he worked, fries were popular. One day someone wasn't pleased because the fries were too thick. Crum made them thinner and thinner until finally, he made fries that were too thin to eat with a fork. The man in the restaurant was happy and people around the world started to eat potato crisps. In the USA, crisps are called 'chips' and in Britain, fries are called 'chips'.

1 Potato crisps are a very popular _____ snack all over the world.

2 A man from _____ invented them.

3 He made the first crisps because a man thought his fries _____.

4 Finally, Crum made fries that were _____ with a fork.

5 Fries are called 'chips' in _____.

13 Join the children with their snacks. Write sentences.

Helen   Katy   Michael

Sarah   David   Robert

1 <u>Helen's favourite snack is bread and butter.</u>

2 _____

3 _____

4 _____

5 _____

6 _____

14 Read the poem. Find the word.

The first letter in 'snack'. I'm hungry, you see. | s |

The second in 'jam'. The fruit's from a tree. | |

The third in 'sausage'. A hot dog to eat. | |

The fourth in 'popcorn'. Salted or sweet. | |

The fifth in 'butter'. I love it on bread. | |

It's something to do with food, I said.

Look at the word and write the letter.

With me, for sure, a dish will taste better.

What am I? _____

15 Read and answer 'yes' or 'no'.

Chopsticks

People in Asia use many different things to eat with, for example hands, spoons, forks, knives and chopsticks.

Chopsticks can be big or small. Most Chinese chopsticks are about 25 cm long. For cooking, they also use longer chopsticks, which can be more than 50 cm long. In Japan chopsticks are shorter and they come to a point at one end.

Chopsticks are made of a number of materials, but most are made of wood or plastic. A long time ago they put silver on the end of the chopsticks.

Things you should or shouldn't do when you eat with chopsticks

- Do not move your chopsticks around.
- Do not pick food up by making a hole in it with your chopsticks.
- Do not pull dishes towards you with chopsticks. Use your hands.
- Pull dishes close to you when eating. Put them back after you use them.
- You can lift your dish up to your mouth to eat small pieces of food.

1 Chopsticks are always long. <u>no</u>____

2 They are the same size in Japan and China. _____

3 They are usually made of plastic or wood. _____

4 Use them to make holes. _____

5 Move your chopsticks a lot. _____

6 Pick your bowl up. _____

16 Match the rhyming words.

1 _c_ enough   **a** water | **6** _h_ cough   **f** caught

2 __ straight   **b** half | **7** __ through   **g** right

3 __ daughter   **c** puff | **8** __ thought   **h** off

4 __ laugh   **d** tights | **9** __ high   **i** zoo

5 __ lights   **e** eight | **10** __ night   **j** why

17 **23 CD2** Listen, check and say.

18 Read and order the instructions.

Bread and tomato snack

Ingredients:

❖ 8 slices of bread   ❖ Olive oil   ❖ 1 piece of garlic

❖ 3 large tomatoes   ❖ 1 small onion   ❖ Black pepper

What you do:

☐ Cover each side of the bread with oil. Take the skin off the garlic and cut it in half.

☐ Then chop the onion into very small pieces. Mix with the tomatoes and a little pepper.

☐ Rub the garlic over both sides of the bread. Place on a metal tray and cook for 15 minutes.

☐ After 15 minutes, take the bread out of the oven. Put some tomato mixture onto each piece of bread. Put it back in the oven for another 5 minutes.

1 Turn the oven on at 200°C.

☐ While that's cooking, take the skin off the tomatoes and then chop them.

A recipe

• A recipe gives instructions so someone can cook something.

• First we include all the food we need. These are the **ingredients**.

• Then we give careful, numbered **instructions** about how to cook the food.

Write it right

19 Look at the ingredients and the pictures. Write the recipe. Use these words.

~~break~~   heat   mix
cut   put

Cold chocolate biscuit cake

1 Break the biscuits into small pieces.

Ingredients:

75 g   25 g   1 tbsp   175 g   200 g

Instructions:

1   **2**   **3**

4   **5**   **6**

20 Read and answer.

1 Why will Diggory have to work quickly? _They've only got enough food for three days._

2 When will Iyam tell Diggory where the Sun Stone is? _____

3 Where are the secret caves? _____

4 Why was corn important to the Mayas and the Aztecs? _____

5 What did the Aztecs eat with chocolate? _____

6 What else did the Aztecs eat? _____

21 Correct the sentences.

1 Emily didn't ask Iyam enough questions.
_Emily asked Iyam too many questions._____

2 There are pictures of sushi on the Sun Stone.
_____

3 Butter was the most important Aztec food.
_____

4 The door to the caves is about three kilometres west.
_____

5 Iyam shouldn't run because the ground is moving.
_____

6 Diggory asked Emily to get him some chopsticks.
_____

? **Do you remember?**

1 We've got too _many_____ strawberries.

2 We haven't got _____ milk.

3 I love butter and strawberry _____ on my bread in the morning.

4 People in China often use _____ to eat with.

5 _____ rhymes with half.

6 After you mix the tomatoes, _____ the mixture on the bread.

Can do   I can use countable and uncountable nouns.
             I can talk about food.
             I can write a recipe.

1 Match the words with the definitions.

1 | y | e | a | s | t |

2 | f | r | i | d | g | e |

3 | m | i | c | r | o | - | o | r | g | a | n | i | s | m |

4 | b | a | c | t | e | r | i | a |

5 | m | o | u | l | d |

6 | y | o | g | h | u | r | t |

a a place where we keep our food cold ☐

b a bad micro-organism which can grow on food ☐

c something we put in bread to make the mixture grow 1

d this is made of milk mixed with bacteria ☐

e a very small living thing ☐

f these can be good or bad and can grow on food ☐

2 Now look at the letters in the grey boxes in Activity **1**. Find a food word.

----

3 Read and match.

1 Keep hot food hot
2 Keep cold food cold
3 Wash fruit and vegetables carefully before you eat or cook them
4 Don't cook with pets in the kitchen
5 Keep meat on the bottom shelf of the fridge

because

a animals can carry bacteria. ☐
b bacteria grow above 5°C. ☐
c bacteria grow below 70°C. 1
d it is colder and meat juices cannot fall onto other food. ☐
e they grow outside where there can be lots of bacteria. ☐

4 Read about an English cheese. Then write about your favourite food from your region.

Stilton cheese is sometimes called 'The King of English cheeses'. It is famous for its strong smell and blue veins. Stilton is made from cow's milk. Only three places in England can make real Stilton cheese: Derbyshire, Nottinghamshire and Leicestershire. It takes about nine weeks to make Stilton and some people keep it for a few more weeks before they eat it. This is because they like the cheese to be softer and even smellier!

My favourite food from my region is ...

5 Look at the three pictures. Write about this story. Write **20** or more words.

....

....

....

....

Review Units ⭐3 and ⭐4

1 Read the story. Choose a word from the box. Write the correct word next to numbers 1–5.

| torch | rucksack | was | too | camp | map | tents | ~~countryside~~ | were | enough |

Friendly

Last week's episode of *Friendly* was really funny because there was a school trip to the <u>countryside</u> . The teachers were taking their pupils to a forest to **(1)** _____ . On Friday afternoon when they were waiting for the bus outside the school, Jenny arrived with a really big, heavy suitcase. She said that her **(2)** _____ wasn't very big and she had lots of equipment.

On the way to the campsite Sally sat next to the bus driver because she wanted to watch her drive, look at the directions and follow them on her **(3)** _____ .

When they got to the forest, all five of them had to help Jenny to pull her suitcase across the field to the **(4)** _____ . The ground was too soft and it was really hard work. When they were pulling the suitcase, it fell over again and again.

It was dinner time when they arrived at the campsite and they were dirty, tired and hungry. Jenny wasn't very pleased when she discovered she couldn't use her hairdryer. She was surprised because she couldn't connect it to any electricity in the wall of the tent! Peter was really unhappy because he wanted to cook sausages and beans, but Jim thought a fire was **(5)** _____ dangerous in a forest. Jim took some peanut butter and jam sandwiches out of his rucksack, Sally said she had some popcorn and biscuits and they all laughed when Sue said she was carrying enough cold sushi and chopsticks for everyone! They all agreed that they were eating the strangest camp menu ever!

2 Now choose the best name for the story.

Tick one box.   A drive in the country ☐   Jenny's big suitcase ☐   Forest fire ☐

3 Which is the odd one out and why?

1 soup   butter   jam   (biscuit)
<u>It's countable.</u> _____

2 chopsticks   fork   torch   spoon
_____

3 best   north   east   south
_____

4 sandwich   sauce   pan   snack
_____

5 tent   cave   sleeping bag   rucksack
_____

6 pasta   bread   cake   cheese
_____

4 Complete the sentences. Count and write the letters.

1 The opposite of east is
west_____. **[4]**

2 We put _____ with
peanut butter in sandwiches. **[ ]**

3 They travelled from Italy
to China. It was a long

_____ . **[ ]**

4 A _____ is like a small
house. We sleep in it when
we camp. **[ ]**

5 A _____ is higher than
a hill. **[ ]**

6 They use _____ to eat
sushi in Japan. **[ ]**

7 We use a _____ to
see in the dark when we go
camping. **[ ]**

8 I don't like this soup. There's
_____ much salt in it. **[ ]**

9 Go from one place to another.

_____ **[ ]**

10 How _____ butter do
we need? **[ ]**

11 A bag which we carry on our
back is a _____ . **[ ]**

12 There were too _____
people at the beach. **[ ]**

13 'What _____ he doing
when he fell?' 'He was skiing.' **[ ]**

14 Something light which we eat
between meals when we're
hungry is a _____ . **[ ]**

15 We only had 50 g of flour. We
didn't have _____ flour
to make biscuits. **[ ]**

5 Write the words in the crossword. Write the message.

1	2	3	4	5	6	7		8	9	10
										t

!

6 Quiz time!

1 When did Alvin break his arm?
When he was _____

2 How did impressionist artists paint?

_____

3 Name an impressionist artist.

_____

4 Why couldn't the kids make the cake?

_____

5 Name two kinds of micro-organism.

_____

6 How do we make yoghurt?

_____

7 Write questions for your quiz in
your notebook.

LOOK again | Present perfect and adverbs

We **still** haven't chosen a project. (= But we have to do it soon.)

The rescue people have been here **since** ten o'clock.
(= When? A point in time: time, date, day, etc.)

It's been here **for** about three hours.
(= How long? How many minutes, hours, days, weeks, etc.)

---

1 Read and choose the right words.

1 Mr Schwarz has taught me German **for** / since / still three years.

2 It hasn't snowed since **three days / Saturday / two weeks**.

3 I **still** / **for** / **since** haven't finished this activity.

4 They **are** / **have** / **were** worked here for a year.

5 She hasn't caught a fish **for** / **since** / **still** two hours.

2 Complete the sentences with 'for' or 'since'.

1 She's lived in her village _since_ 2008.

2 My little brother has studied English _____ six months.

3 I haven't seen Peter _____ Monday.

4 Mum has had her favourite jacket _____ ten years!

5 I haven't eaten anything _____ nine o'clock.

3 Look at the code (a = ___). Write the secret message.

a	b	c		j	k	l		s	t	u
d	e	f		m	n	o		v	w	x
g	h	i		p	q	r		y	z	

_I_ _'_ _v_ _e_ _____ _____ _____ _____

_____ _____ _____ _____ _____ _____ _____ _____

_____ _____ _____ _____ _____ _____

_____ _____ _____ _____ _____ _____ _____ _____ _____

_____ _____ _____ _____ _____ _____ _____ _____ .

4 Write a message in code in your notebook.

5 Find and write four sentences.

liked fishing	three o'clock.	this lesson since
in that flat for	five years.	We've been in
~~He's loved~~	I've	for nine months.
started school.	They've lived	~~maths since he~~

He's loved maths since he _____

_____

_____

_____

6 Write sentences about you with 'for' or 'since'.

1 (this room)   I've been in this room for ten minutes.
2 (this class) _____
3 (best friend) _____
4 (this school) _____
5 (my house) _____
6 (English) _____

7 Use the ideas in Activity 6 to write questions to ask your friend.

1 How long have you been in this room?
2 _____
3 _____
4 _____
5 _____
6 _____

8 Read and complete the table.

It's 12 o'clock. There are four children on a bus. Peter was the first boy on the bus. He's been on the bus for ten minutes now, but he's going to get off at the next stop, in two minutes.

David was the last to get on. He got on two minutes ago, but he's going to get off last.

Helen has been on the bus for four minutes. She's going to get off at the same stop as Emma.

Emma has been on the bus for the same time as Helen. She's going to get off at the stop after Peter, in four minutes' time.

Helen and Emma are going to get off the bus seven minutes before David.

	Got on the bus?	Going to get off the bus?	How long on the bus in total?
Peter	11.50		
David			
Helen			
Emma			

9 Complete the crossword.

¹J e l ²l y f i ³s h

10 Write the words.

1 Big ones have got the biggest eyes in the world. _squid_____

2 It's got eight legs, but it hasn't got a shell.
_____

3 It has no brain or bones but it eats tiny fish and animals.
_____

4 The salt water which covers Earth.
_____

5 It's got eight legs, two claws and a hard shell. It walks from side to side.
_____

6 It's a mammal which lives in the sea. It isn't a dolphin or a whale.
_____

7 It's a sea animal that forms reefs.
_____

8 It's a sea animal with big claws and a hard shell. _____

11 Read the text. Write the words.

(1) _Fishing____ is a very important activity. Every year people eat more than 100 million

tonnes of (2) _____ (one tonne is a thousand kilos). That's a lot of fish, so we need

to be careful and not catch too many.

People don't only eat fish though. In different countries people eat lots of other sea creatures.

Inuit people eat (3) _____ , and (4) _____ and

(5) _____ are favourite foods in Japan and Greece. (6) _____

are popular all over the world and people pay a lot of (7) _____ to eat

(8) _____ in some countries, for example the USA and France.

12 Circle twelve words. Which two are different? Why?

beautifu l oud angeroustrongreaturtlexcitedolphinicexcitingoodirty

_____ and _____ are different. They are _____ .

13 Compare these sea animals. Use adjectives from Activity 12 and your own ideas.

1 jellyfish – seals _____ Jellyfish are more dangerous than seals. _____

2 coral – an octopus _____

3 an octopus – a jellyfish _____

4 turtles – lobsters _____

5 a whale – a squid _____

6 a shark – a crab _____

14 Read and colour and write.

Find the octopus which is sitting on the big rock. Colour it purple. Next, look for the squid. There are three. Colour the smallest squid yellow. At the bottom of the picture there's a lot of coral. Colour the coral red. Have you found the lobster? It's in the bottom left corner of the picture. Write 'lobster' above it. At the top of the picture there are some jellyfish. Colour the biggest one blue. There's only one more animal to colour. It's the crab. There are three crabs, but only colour the crab which is inside the big shell. Colour it pink.

15 Read and match.

1 The world's first coral reef

2 Storms can

3 Scientists have used coral reefs

4 When parrot fish eat coral,

5 The biggest reef in the world

a is the Great Barrier Reef in Australia.

b appeared about 500 million years ago.

c they make beautiful white sand.

d to make a lot of different medicines.

e break coral reefs.

1

16 Write the words in the columns.

waited ~~invited~~ waterfall enough understand
cinema magazine eaten between important
about octopus coral explorer engineer

① ••	② ••	③ •••	④ •••	⑤ •••
waited				

17 🔊 34 CD2 Listen, check and say.

18 Read and complete the factfile.

Seahorses are one of the sea's most interesting animals. They are small fish but their head looks like a horse.

They are different from most other fish because they don't have scales. They have thin skin over the top of bones. There are over 32 kinds of seahorse, which are different sizes and live in different parts of the world. They can live in coral reefs or in water which is not very deep. They swim slowly and can change their colour so that other fish don't eat them. Seahorses eat small fish and krill.

The biggest seahorses can be up to 30 cm long, and the smallest isn't longer than 3 cm from head to tail.

I think they are the most beautiful sea animal.

Write it right

A report
• When you write a report you first need to organise the information.
• Make a factfile with your information. Include interesting facts.
• Give your report a structure: Introduction – Body – Conclusion

FACTFILE – SEAHORSES

Body: small, head like a horse

Different kinds: _____

Where: _____

How move: _____

Food: _____

Interesting fact: _____

_____

19 Make a sea animal factfile in your notebook. Write a report.

20 Read and answer.

1 What has Emily found? <u>She has found a torch.</u>

2 What did Quetzalcoatl get at Teotihuacan? _____

3 What kind of shell has Diggory seen? _____

4 Why is Iyam like this animal? _____

5 Was gold a treasure for the Aztecs? _____

6 What is Richard going to do if they don't help Iyam? _____

21 Write sentences from the story.

1 You / pull / these plants / and / you / open / this cave
   <u>You've pulled these plants and you've opened this cave.</u>

2 I / find / a torch
   _____

3 I / know / about / these caves / 1971
   _____

4 This / be / the place / their gods / make / the Sun / the Moon / the universe
   _____

5 There / be / gold here / hundreds of years
   _____

6 Richard / use / my mobile / follow us
   _____

? **Do you remember?**

1 I've been here <u>since</u>_____ seven o'clock.

2 She's lived in this town _____ five years.

3 The Pacific _____ is the biggest in the world.

4 I think _____ reefs are really beautiful.

5 Engineer has _____ syllables and the stress is at the _____ of the word.

6 Seahorses can change _____ .

Can do   I can talk about things that have happened using *for* and *since*.

I can talk about sea animals.

I can write a report about sea animals.

1 **Read and label the pictures.**

In the Arctic the biggest land animal, and the top predator on land, is the polar bear. Their favourite food is seals, but they sometimes eat small beluga whales if the whales can't move in the Arctic ice. There are many different kinds of seals in the Arctic and they eat a lot of sea animals. The most important food for seals is fish. Most of the fish eat zooplankton and the zooplankton lives by eating phytoplankton.

| seal   zooplankton   ~~phytoplankton~~   polar bear   fish |

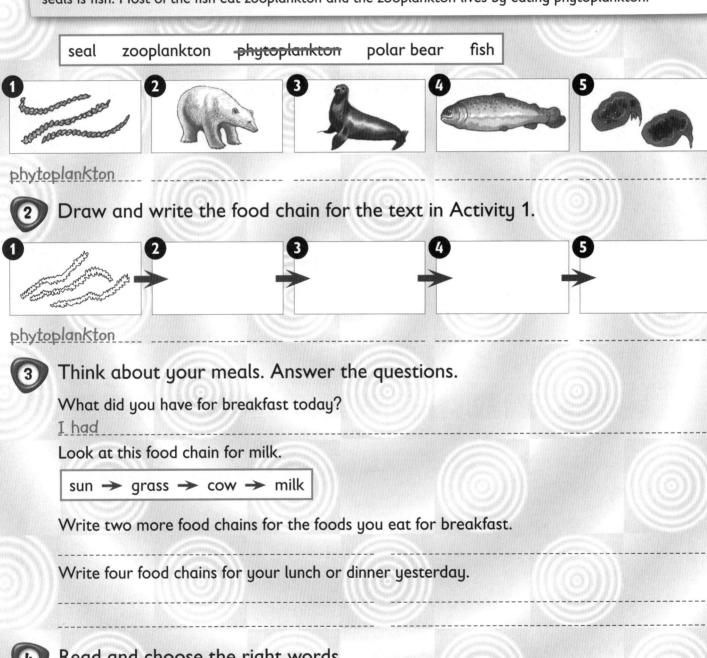

1 **2** **3** **4** **5**

phytoplankton

2 **Draw and write the food chain for the text in Activity 1.**

1 → **2** → **3** → **4** → **5**

phytoplankton

3 **Think about your meals. Answer the questions.**

What did you have for breakfast today?
I had

Look at this food chain for milk.

| sun → grass → cow → milk |

Write two more food chains for the foods you eat for breakfast.

Write four food chains for your lunch or dinner yesterday.

4 **Read and choose the right words.**

1 Eagles eat **snakes** / **corn** / **grass**.

2 Snakes eat **flour** / **turtles** / **lizards**.

3 Lizards eat **fish** / **insects** / **birds**.

4 Insects eat **fish** / **plants** / **mice**.

Use your answers to write a land food chain.
plants →

5 **Sarah is talking to her friend, Katy. What does Katy say to Sarah?**

Read the conversation and choose the best answer.
Write a letter (A–E) for each answer.
There is one example.

Example

Sarah:	Hi Katy! I haven't seen you for a long time.
Katy:	C_____

Questions

1 Sarah: That's nice. Did you go anywhere interesting?
   Katy: _____

2 Sarah: Oh! I haven't been there. Did you like it?
   Katy: _____

3 Sarah: I'll ask my mum to take me next week.
   Katy: _____

4 Sarah: Which is the best day to go, do you think?
   Katy: _____

A   Yes, it was great. There were lots of things to do.

B   Friday. That's when you can swim with the dolphins.

C   I know. I've been on holiday. **(Example)**

D   Yes. I went to the 'Sea Life' centre.

E   That's a good idea.

LOOK again Quantifiers

some	any	no	every
someone	**any**one	**no**-one	**every**one
something	**any**thing	**no**thing	**every**thing
somewhere	**any**where	**no**where	**every**where

1 Read the test carefully. Follow the instructions.

Reading Test

1 First read ALL the instructions.

2 Write the name of someone you like.

----

3 Think of somewhere you like going.

----

4 Name something you can use to write.

----

5 Write your full name.

----

6 Write somewhere you can sleep.

----

7 Only write the answers to numbers 5 and 8.

----

8 Name someone who teaches you.

----

2 Read and choose the right words.

1 I can't see (**anything**) / **something**.

2 Is there **everywhere** / **anywhere** I can sit down?

3 I couldn't find my book and I looked **everywhere** / **somewhere**.

4 Can **no-one** / **anyone** give me a pencil, please?

5 Have you got **nothing** / **anything** made of plastic?

6 **Everyone** / **Anyone** stand up, please.

3 Read and complete.

anyone	everywhere
everywhere	inside
~~no-one~~	no-one

A man is watching TV when he hears the door. He opens it but (1) no-one is there. He looks (2) _____ : to the left, to the right, up and finally he looks down and he sees a snail. He's angry so he picks up the snail and throws it really hard.

He then goes back (3) _____ his house.

    A month later, the same thing happens. He opens the door but there isn't (4) _____ there. He looks (5) _____ , but there's (6) _____ there. Finally he looks down and sees the snail again. He picks it up, but before he can throw it again, the snail says, 'Why did you do that?'

4 Tell the story in the past. Write it in your notebook.

5 Read and answer.

1 In this sport everyone wears boots. There are 11 players in a team and anyone can kick something which is round. Not everyone can catch the round thing. Only one player can do that.

a What's the thing which they kick?
A ball.

b What's the sport? _ _ _ _ _ _ _ _ _ _ _ _ _ _

c Who are the people who play this sport?

_ _ _ _ _ _ _ _ _ _ _ _ _ _

2 In this sport someone puts some long things on their feet and goes to the top of a hill or a mountain. They go down the hill over something which is cold and white.

a What are the long things which they put on their feet? _ _ _ _ _ _ _ _ _ _ _ _ _ _

b What are they doing? _ _ _ _ _ _ _ _ _ _ _ _ _ _

c What's the thing which is cold and white?

_ _ _ _ _ _ _ _ _ _ _ _ _ _

3 In this sport everyone uses something long to hit something which is very small and round. No-one can kick, catch or throw the small, round thing. They have to hit it into a small hole.

a What's the sport? _ _ _ _ _ _ _ _ _ _ _ _ _ _

b Do you play it inside or outside?

_ _ _ _ _ _ _ _ _ _ _ _ _ _

c Where is the hole? _ _ _ _ _ _ _ _ _ _ _ _ _ _

6 Write a definition for a sport or a hobby. Use the words from the 'Look' box on Pupil's Book page 54.

_ _
_ _
_ _
_ _
_ _

7 Match the sentences with the pictures.

~~**a** Would anyone like to play tennis?~~
b Let's go somewhere different on holiday this year.
c No-one wants to play soccer today.
d There's nowhere for us to play.

1

2
a

3

4

8 Read and order the text.

☐ could do it, but No-one did it. Someone was angry, because really it was

☐ do it, but No-one thought that Everyone wasn't going to do it.

☐ In the end Everyone was really angry with Someone when No-one did what Anyone could do.

1 Once upon a time there were four children in a class. Their names

☐ Their teacher asked for some help in the classroom. Everyone thought that Someone was going to do it.

☐ It wasn't difficult, so Anyone something that Everyone could do. Everyone thought that Anyone could

☐ were No-one, Anyone, Someone and Everyone.

9 Label the photos.

1 b e a t b o x
4 _ _ _ _ _

2 _ _ _ _ _ _ _ _ _ _ _ _ _

5 _ _ _ _ _ _ _ _ _ _ _ _

3 _ _ _ _ _ _ _ _ _ _

10 Follow the free time words.

hobby	does	free running	sewing	playing the piano	baseball
clothes design	to	beatbox	Someone	different	chess
skateboarding	places	table tennis	bored.	goes	skating
mountain biking	things	cooking	interesting	never	reading
board games	skiing	golf	and	is	who

11 Look at the other words in Activity 10. Use them to write a sentence.

Someone _____

_____

12 Read and answer.

When people first started free running, they did it to get from one place to another using the quickest path. They ran and jumped from wall to wall, and down steps. Now they try to do it in the most beautiful way possible.

In Britain, free running became popular in 2003 after someone made a TV programme about it.

Free running has also been on a music video by the pop star Madonna. We can see it in action films and adverts on TV, and there is also a 'Free running' video game.

It is important to remember that it is something which not everyone can do because free runners need to be very strong and fit. It is also difficult and it can be dangerous.

1 When did free running become popular in Britain? In 2003. _____

2 Which pop star used free running in her music video? _____

3 Where else can you see free running? _____

4 Can everyone do free running? _____

5 Why / Why not? _____

13 Find four differences.

In picture a, two boys are playing chess. In picture b, they are girls.

14 Read the email. Choose the right words and write them on the lines.

Hi Mary,

How are you? Did **(1)** you have a good holiday? **(2)** _____ was great. I went to a special activity camp and I've started some new hobbies. **(3)** _____ was at the camp for five days and **(4)** _____ did something different every day! The first two days it was raining so we did puzzles, played board games and I learned to play chess. I also designed some clothes!

On Wednesday they took **(5)** _____ to the hills where we rode amazing mountain bikes. It was really exciting. Pete taught **(6)** _____ how to skateboard on Thursday morning so I spent all afternoon skateboarding with my friends. Friday was **(7)** _____ last day and we did beatbox and rap!

(8) _____ only problem now is that I have too many hobbies!
Emma

1	they	you	us
2	Mine	I	You
3	He	We	I
4	him	we	them
5	we	they	us
6	me	her	you
7	his	me	our
8	I	Me	My

15 Write questions for the answers.

1 Where did she go?
She went to an activity camp.

2 _____
She was there for five days.

3 _____
Because it was raining.

4 _____
She learned to play chess.

5 _____
They rode amazing mountain bikes.

6 _____
They did beatbox and rap.

16 Write an email to a friend about your hobbies in your notebook.

17 Complete the sentences.

cousin	someone	done	~~love~~
doesn't	touch	nothing	country

1 We __love__ going to London.
2 Germany is a big _____ .
3 Can _____ answer this question?
4 Please don't _____ the animals at the zoo.
5 My _____ is coming for lunch.
6 My brother _____ like catching buses.
7 Have you _____ your homework yet?
8 I've opened the box and there's _____ inside it.

18 [10 CD3] Listen, check and say.

19 Read the review and answer.

Yesterday I listened to Bruce Star's new single, 'Happily Happy'. This is the second song from Bruce's new CD 'Bigger', which came into the shops at the start of February. In my opinion, this is the best song Bruce has written since he left his old band 'The Starlets'. I love the chorus, when he repeats 'Happily Happy', and I think he sings the song beautifully. I also like the drums, which are strong and loud. The only thing I don't like much is the sound of the guitar. I think it sounds too fast. I prefer it when he plays the guitar more slowly.

Expressing opinions
In my opinion …
I like / love …
I think / don't think …
I prefer …

Write it right

1 What's the song called? 'Happily Happy'. _____
2 Who sang it? _____
3 What album is it from? _____
4 What does the writer like most about it? _____
5 What else does she like? _____
6 What doesn't she like and why? _____

20 Think of your favourite song. Answer the questions in your notebook.

- What's the song called? • Who sang it? • What album is it from?
- What else do you like? • What do you like most? • Is there anything you don't like?

21 Now write a review in your notebook.

I'm going to review _____

22 Read and answer.

1 Where are they going to go?
<u>Somewhere nearer the sea.</u>

2 What will take Iyam to a cave of gold?
----

3 Are Kukulcan and Quetzalcoatl the same?
----

4 What's Kukulcan's temple called?
----

5 What did the Mayas do before their ball game?
----

6 In what months can you see the snake on the stairs?
----

23 Look at the code. Write the secret message in your notebook.

> N = north   S = south   E = east   W = west

Tlachtli – 5E – 4S – 2W – 3N – 3W – 3S – 4E – 4N – 1S – 3W – 3S – 2N – 4E – 2W – 2N –
1W – 4S – 1N – 2W – 5E – 2N – 3W – 1S – 2W – 4E – 1S – 1W – 2W – 3N.

Tlachtli	walls.	ball	rubber	played.	was
which	had	stone	game	They	of
up	pass	high	heavy	in	a
circle	the	a	of	one	made
Mayan	to	through	ball	men	a

? **Do you remember?**

1 Is there <u>anywhere</u> _____ I can sit down?
2 I've looked _____ but I can't find my pen.
3 _____ is a very old board game.
4 Music and rhythm which you make with your mouth is called _____ .
5 Spain is my favourite _____ .
6 In my _____ , pop music is the best kind of music.

Can do   I can talk about *something, anything,*
nothing and *everything.*
I can talk about different hobbies.
I can write a song review.

1 Do the music questionnaire.

1 What kind of music do you like? _____

2 How often do you listen to music? _____

3 Who's your favourite singer? _____

4 Which is your favourite group? _____

5 How do you listen to music? (radio, MP3, mobile phone, etc.) _____

6 Do you buy music from the internet? _____

2 Ask someone else the questions. Write about your answers in your notebook.

My dad likes opera, but I don't. We both _____

3 Read and answer the questions.

Louis Armstrong was a famous trumpet player and jazz singer. Louis was born in 1901 in New Orleans in the USA. His family didn't have much money so after he left school at the age of 11, he sang with a group of boys to get money. He started playing the trumpet at the same age and at 14 he was working in his first band. During his life Armstrong played the trumpet and sang with all the world's best musicians. He was famous for his improvisation and the way he played the melodies. In some songs his singing sounds like a trumpet, with no words.

1 What was Louis's surname?
Armstrong. _____

2 When was he born?
_____

3 Where was he born?
_____

4 How old was he when he left school?
_____

5 When did he start playing the trumpet?
_____

6 What was he famous for?
_____

4 Look at this factfile for Biz Markie. Write a report.

FACTFILE

Name: Marcel Hall

Born: 8 April, 1964, in New York

School: Long Island High School

First job: DJ in New York clubs – new name Biz Markie

First record: 1985 single 'Def Fresh Crew'

Musical style: hip hop, rap and beatbox

Other jobs: actor in the film 'Meteor Man'

Biz Markie's real name

5 **Read the story. Choose a word from the box. Write the correct word next to numbers 1–5. There is one example.**

Example				
~~help~~	them	playing	basement	space
often	plays	want	parents	countryside

Rachel and Paul <u>help</u>_____ at an animal rescue centre in their free time. They
(1) _____ go there at the weekend. They love (2) _____ with the dogs
and cats. They also help to look after (3) _____ . They give the animals their food
and clean their boxes. They love doing this because they love animals.

They sometimes go to a special market with their (4) _____ and other grown-ups. At
the market they sell things to get money for the rescue centre and to ask other people to help. One
day a rich and famous actor went to the rescue centre and took two big dogs and three cats home
to his house in the (5) _____ . He lives in a castle!

(6) Now choose the best name for the story.

Tick one box.

Friends and family   ☐

Pet rescue   ☐

A day at the market   ☐

Review Units ⭐5 and ⭐6

1 Read the story. Choose a word from the box. Write the correct word next to numbers 1–5.

ridden	someone	~~hobbies~~	chess	cook	nowhere	dangerous
anything	squid	ocean				

Friendly

In today's episode the friends are talking about the <u>hobbies</u> that they do in their free time. Jim's started free running and is really excited about it. He says he got the idea when he saw the film *The Harder They Run* and the actor, Bruce Willis, had to run through a city centre. Sally says she loves action films and that there are special actors who do all the tricks. Her favourite is Max Limit. Max has driven cars at over 200 kilometres an hour, he's flown lots of different planes and he's
(1) _____ motorbikes, horses and elephants. Jenny doesn't find any of this exciting and she tells Jim that she thinks his new hobby is strange and too **(2)** _____ .

Sue's hobby isn't dangerous, but once when she was painting a small waterfall in the countryside, she fell into the river, which was moving very fast, and **(3)** _____ had to pull her out. Peter loves trying new things to eat. He says he'll try anything. He's eaten octopus and **(4)** _____ before, but on his last holiday in Japan, he and his parents ate blowfish. This fish is very, very poisonous and someone has to prepare and cook it very well or you can die when you eat it. Jenny tries to remember the most dangerous thing she's ever done. Jim laughs because he can't believe she's ever done **(5)** _____ dangerous. Jenny says that once she ate one of Sue's dishes and everyone knows that she's a terrible cook!

2 Now choose the best name for the story.

Tick one box.   Living dangerously ☐   Hard actors ☐   Eating seafood ☐

3 Which is the odd one out and why?

1 golf (badminton) soccer tennis
<u>You don't play it with a ball.</u>

2 seen ridden walked thought
_____

3 baseball volleyball soccer basketball
_____

4 crab jellyfish lobster turtle
_____

5 skates skis chess skateboards
_____

6 laughed arrived remembered turned
_____

4 Complete the sentences. Count and write the letters.

1 'How many fish has that dolphin
   _eaten_____ ?' 'Six.'   `5`

2 In _____ people run
   and jump through a city centre.   ☐

3 A sea animal without claws
   which has got eight legs. It isn't
   a squid. _____   ☐

4 _____ is a black and
   white board game.   ☐

5 An _____ is usually
   bigger than seas, rivers
   and lakes.   ☐

6 'Is there _____ in the
   café?' 'No, everyone's gone.'   ☐

7 A _____ is something
   hard on the outside of an
   animal's body. A turtle's
   got one.   ☐

8 We stand on a _____
   to go fast in parks.   ☐

9 A _____ is a round
   animal with eight legs and two
   arms with claws.   ☐

10 He's been a footballer
   _____ 2005.   ☐

11 _____ looks like a little
   forest but it's lots of sea animals.   ☐

12 A _____ is in the same
   family as dolphins and seals,
   but it's much bigger.   ☐

13 A bat is _____ which
   we use to hit a ball.   ☐

14 'How long have you _____
   your mountain bike?' 'A year.'   ☐

15 He's been a photographer
   _____ nine years.   ☐

5 Write the words in the crossword. Write the message.

(crossword grid with clues numbered 1–8, including the across entry filled in: e a t e n)

1	2	3	3		4	5	6	3		1	7	8
												n !

6 Quiz time!

1 What were the people rescuing
  on the beach?
  They were _____

2 Why are plants called 'producers'?
  _____

3 What is a top predator?
  _____

4 What is the music behind the tune?
  _____

5 How old is opera?
  _____

7 Write questions for your quiz in your notebook.

7 Dress Sense

LOOK again | Possibility

I think it **may look** better with a jacket.   I **might buy** a new jacket.

I **might not** need a jacket.

1 Write the clothes words in alphabetical order.

trousers	~~bracelet~~	sweater	jacket	glasses	dress	watch	coat	skirt
T-shirt	hat	jeans	shirt	handbag	shoes	scarf	socks	trainers

bracelet, _____

_____

_____

_____

2 Read and choose the right words.

1 He (**may buy**) / **may buys** / **may to buy** some new trainers.

2 She **mights wear** / **might wears** / **might wear** her gold bracelet.

3 It **not might** / **might not** / **isn't might** be cold.

4 You **may prefer** / **mays prefer** / **may prefers** olives on your pizza.

5 They **can't might** / **might not** / **don't might** win this afternoon's game.

6 You **might** / **must** / **can** need a scarf because I think it's cold outside!

3 Write about your clothes.

1 My trainers are made of _____ .

2 My jacket is made of _____ .

3 My shoes _____ .

4 Tomorrow I might wear _____ because _____ .

5 At the weekend I might wear _____ because _____ .

4 Complete the sentences.

go	visit	~~wear~~	get	get up	watch

1 He might wear a jacket this afternoon because it's cold.

2 She might _____ TV after lunch.

3 They might _____ us today.

4 You might not _____ your present until Sunday.

5 I may not _____ shopping tomorrow.

6 We may _____ early on Saturday.

5 What do you think it is? Use 'may'.

1 It may be _____ **2** _____ **3** _____ **4** _____

_____ _____ _____ _____

6 Look at the picture. Read and answer 'yes' or 'no'.

1 They might have a picnic. yes _____
2 She might be lost. _____
3 He may want to catch a bus home. _____
4 She might not be happy. _____
5 It might rain. _____
6 They might need coats. _____

7 Correct the sentences.

1 They mights wear their jeans. They might wear their jeans. _____
2 She does might take a jacket. _____
3 I don't might put on my sweater. _____
4 Peter may plays football tomorrow. _____
5 I might not to wear my black shoes. _____
6 They mays wear their new trainers. _____

8 Find and write five sentences.

Susan	might put	is green	coats and scarves.
Our school	took	of	and red.
Richard	uniform	on their	plastic.
My schoolbag's	wore her	blue spotted	with him.
The children	made	a jacket	belt.

1 Susan wore her blue spotted belt. _____
2 _____
3 _____
4 _____
5 _____

9 Find two words for each group of letters. One is a clothes word.

1 tr- <u>trainers</u> , <u>traffic</u>
2 sh- _____ , _____
3 po- _____ , _____
4 gl- _____ , _____
5 u-   _____ , _____
6 bu- _____ , _____

mbrella · oves · ~~ainers~~ · ue · orts · gly · tter · ~~affic~~ · opping · tato · cket · tton

10 Label the photos with words from Activity 9.

1 2 3 4 5 6

<u>pocket</u> _____ _____ _____ _____ _____

11 Read and complete the sentences with 1, 2, 3 or 4 words.

Last Saturday Jane went shopping with her Aunt Helen to buy some new clothes. They went to three different clothes shops. The first shop was called Legs Eleven and they had lots of socks. Jane chose some grey and green ones.

Next they went to look for some shorts. They found lots in a shop called 4 Fashion. Jane didn't know which ones to choose, so her aunt helped her. She got a lovely blue pair made of cotton, with big pockets.

In the last clothes shop they bought a beautiful red coat. She didn't buy any new trainers because she's got three pairs at home. When they were coming home, it started to rain so they bought two umbrellas from a small shop. They caught the bus home because they didn't want to get wet.

1 Jane went to the shops with <u>her Aunt Helen.</u> _____
2 Legs Eleven was _____ shop which they went into.
3 Jane's new socks are _____ .
4 Aunt Helen helped Jane _____ some shorts.
5 Jane's new blue shorts are made of _____ and they have big pockets.
6 She didn't need _____ because she's got three pairs.
7 They got _____ in the last clothes shop.
8 They went home on _____ because it was raining.

12 **Read and complete the circle with names and clothes words.**

Three girls and two boys are sitting round a table. Richard is sitting between two girls. The girl on his left is called Emma.

The girl on William's left is called Betty.

The girl between Richard and Sarah is wearing a striped T-shirt and a skirt. She has a beautiful gold ring.

The boy with the shorts is wearing a belt. He's also wearing a shirt and a new jacket.

The girl with the scarf isn't wearing a skirt. She's wearing some trousers and a sweater which is made of cotton.

The girl on the right of Richard has got some plastic earrings on. She's also wearing a striped sweater, a skirt and trainers.

The other boy is cold so he's wearing some gloves. His sweater is striped and he's also wearing trousers.

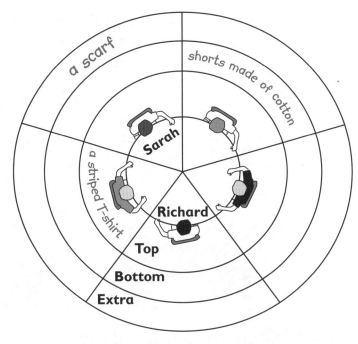

13 **Draw a piece of clothing and write about it.**

These are my favourite long shorts. They're very, very big so I wear them with a belt. They're dark brown and they've got big pockets on the legs above the knees. My mum hates them, but I love them!

14 **Describe the picture.**

1 No-one is playing chess. _____

2 Nothing _____
_____ .

3 No-one _____
_____ .

4 Everyone _____
_____ .

15 Match the sentences with the pictures. Write letters a–f.

> **a** I'm angry. Please stop talking!   **b** I'm on holiday. I'm happy!
> **c** I'm excited! This is a fantastic present!   **d** What a surprise!
> **e** I'm tired. Goodnight, Mum.   **f** I'm sad. I've hurt my knee.

16 🔊 23 CD3 Listen, check and say.

17 Look at the pictures. Read and tick (✓) the correct picture.

> There are two people in the picture: a man and a woman. The man is taller than the woman, but she's got longer hair. The man's got dark, curly hair and a small beard, but he hasn't got a moustache. He's wearing a long coat over the top of a pair of black trousers and a shirt. He's got black shoes on. He looks like a detective. He's standing next to a woman who's got long, curly, blonde hair. She's got big eyes and a long, thin nose. She's smiling. She's wearing jeans, a short jacket and trainers. She looks like a rock star.

Describing people
Describe their face and body.
→ He's got a big nose and long, brown, curly hair.
Describe their clothes.
→ She's wearing a beautiful, long, blue, cotton skirt.
Describe what they look like.
→ He looks like an angry chef.

Write it right

18 Now write a description in your notebook of one of the other pictures. Can your friend guess which picture it is?

19 Read and answer.

1 What did Aztec braves wear? <u>They wore birds' feathers and animal fur.</u>

2 How did everyone feel when they saw them? _____

3 What did the Mayas do in the round building? _____

4 Why do they have to move fast? _____

5 When do the bowls work like mirrors? _____

6 At what time is the Sun at its highest? _____

20 Put the verbs into the past simple.

The Aztecs **(1)** <u>were</u> _____ (are) very rich. They **(2)** _____ (have) fields and water to grow

plants for food and materials. They also **(3)** _____ (have) lots of stone for building, and gold and

silver. Like the Mayas, they **(4)** _____ (get) the liquid from rubber trees and **(5)** _____

(use) that too. They **(6)** _____ (make) balls for their famous ball game and **(7)** _____

(use) it to clean their teeth after meals. They **(8)** _____ (invent) the first chewing gum!

Rich Aztec people **(9)** _____ (wear) more clothes than poor people, and their clothes

(10) _____ (are) made from different cloth. Poor people **(11)** _____ (can't) wear

cotton. Women and girls **(12)** _____ (make) most of their cloth from the 'century plant' and

(13) _____ (use) bright colours and designs to decorate it. They **(14)** _____ (make)

shoes from rubber, but if they **(15)** _____ (have) to go into a temple or see the king, they

(16) _____ (can't) wear anything on their feet. When they **(17)** _____ (dance), they

(18) _____ (wear) belts with sea shells to make music as they **(19)** _____ (move).

They sometimes **(20)** _____ (wear) feathers and animal fur too. Aztec braves

(21) _____ (paint) their faces to look horrible and to make people afraid of them. Married

women **(22)** _____ (put) their hair up on top of their heads. Corn **(23)** _____ (is)

their most important food, but they also **(24)** _____ (eat) a lot of vegetables. They

(25) _____ (don't eat) a lot of meat, but they sometimes **(26)** _____ (eat) insects

and lizards.

? **Do you remember?**

1 It might <u>rain</u> _____ later so I'm going to take an umbrella.

2 I need to study because we _____ have a maths test tomorrow, but I'm not sure.

3 I've got a new _____ so my trousers don't fall down.

4 When it's cold, I wear _____ on my hands.

5 My brother is very _____ because it's his birthday party tonight.

6 That man with the long coat looks _____ a detective.

Can do   I can talk about possibility using *may* and *might*.

I can talk about clothes.

I can write a description of someone and their clothes.

History · Clothes

1 Label the picture.

belt	gloves	jacket
~~scarf~~	pocket	helmet
trousers	boots	

1 scarf
2 _____
3 _____
4 _____
5 _____
6 _____
7 _____
8 _____

2 Complete the text about the fire fighter's uniform. Use words from Activity 1.

This fire fighter's uniform is made from special materials to protect him at work. The **(1)** helmet_____ hasn't changed much in the last 150 years. It is made of leather and it protects the fire fighter's head.

   Below the fire fighter's face he wears a **(2)** _____. It's made of cotton and he can pull it up over his head in a fire.

   The fire fighter's jacket has a special **(3)** _____ at the front. He uses this to carry his radio or his gloves.

   The fire fighter wears **(4)** _____ which are bigger than usual. He must put them on quickly over his boots when he needs to go and fight a fire. They have a plastic stripe at the bottom so people can see him in the dark. His **(5)** _____ are made of leather and metal. They are very strong.

   One of the most important parts of the uniform is the fire fighter's **(6)** _____. They are made of leather and they protect his hands.

3 Label the activities and sports. Write about two of the uniforms.

1
2
3
4
5

dancing_____ _____ _____ _____ _____

This man is wearing special clothes for playing sport.

4 🔲 26 CD3 **Listen and tick (✓) the box. There is one example.**

What has Holly put on to go to the park?

A ✓   B ☐   C ☐

1   Where has Richard left his umbrella?

A ☐   B ☐   C ☐

2   Where is William going to go for his holiday?

A ☐   B ☐   C ☐

3   Which trousers will Emma wear to the party?

A ☐   B ☐   C ☐

4   Where is Helen's brown belt now?

A ☐   B ☐   C ☐

LOOK again | Present perfect and adverbs

| Have you finished **yet**? | I've **just** finished this book. |
| I haven't finished **yet**. | I've **already** finished my project. |

1 Find two irregular past participles for each group of letters.

1 b- *been* , *begun*
2 m- _____ , _____
3 dr- _____ , _____
4 t- _____ , _____
5 th- _____ , _____
6 br- _____ , _____

7 sp- _____ , _____
8 l- _____ , _____
9 c- _____ , _____
10 st- _____ , _____
11 r- _____ , _____
12 go- _____ , _____

aken
awn   ost
ne
oken
idden
iven

aught   ome   ood   ought   eant   ent   ~~een~~   eft
olen   aught   rown
un   oken   t   ought   ~~egun~~   et

2 Complete the sentences with verbs from Activity 1.

1 He's r*idden* his bike for two hours.
2 They've just g_____ out.
3 This is the third time I've b_____ to read this book!

4 She hasn't s_____ all her money yet.
5 Our cat still hasn't c_____ home.
6 They've just d_____ a picture.

3 Look at the picture. Write sentences.

1 (get up) *He's already got up.*
2 (tidy his room) *He hasn't tidied his room yet.*
3 (make his bed) _____
4 (put on his shoes) _____
5 (have breakfast) _____
6 (put on his trousers) _____

Come on! Time for breakfast!

4 Write sentences about you today. Use 'already', 'yet' or 'just'.

1 (have lunch) *I've already had lunch. / I haven't had lunch yet. / I've just had lunch.*
2 (read something) _____
3 (do some of my homework) _____
4 (listen to music) _____

5 Tick (✓) two more correct sentences. Correct two more sentences.

1 'Tidy your room!' 'I've already tidied it!' ✓
2 He is done his homework already. _He's already done his homework._
3 Has he been to Australia?
4 I live here for ten years.
5 They's seen that film already.
6 She's studied English for three years.

6 What have they just done?

He's just tidied his room. She_____. They_____.

She_____. We_____. He_____.

7 Look at the Hirds' plans. Read and answer 'Yes, they have' or 'No, they haven't'.

HOLIDAY!		morning	afternoon
Monday	Cambridge	see the university	play in a park
Tuesday	Nottingham	see the castle	walk in Sherwood Forest
Wednesday	Liverpool	cross the River Mersey	go shopping
Thursday	York	walk on the Roman walls	visit the Viking Museum
Friday	London	visit the Science Museum	see Big Ben

Now it is Wednesday lunchtime.
1 The Hirds haven't been to Cambridge yet. _Yes, they have._
2 They have already seen Nottingham Castle.
3 They have already been shopping in Liverpool.
4 They haven't visited the Science Museum yet.
5 They've already walked in Sherwood Forest.
6 They haven't played in a park in Cambridge yet.

8 Label the car stickers with nationalities. Use the letters in the box.

(E)   (BR)

```
ɑ a a a a a c c d
e e e e e e e g h
h i̶ i i i k l m n̶
n n n n n o p̶ r
r r r r s̶ s t u u x
z B F G G I M P S̶
```

(IND)   (F)

1 Spanish _____   2 _____

5 _____   6 _____

(GR)   (P)

(D)   (MEX)

3 _____   4 _____

7 _____   8 _____

9 What countries are these web pages from?

www.mundocrianças.br	1 Brazil _____	www.kidsofindia.in	5 _____
www.kinderhere.de	2 _____	www.sunfun4kids.gr	6 _____
www.niñolandia.es	3 _____	www.4crianças.pt	7 _____
www.mondenfant.fr	4 _____	www.mundoniños.mx	8 _____

10 Read and answer.

Did you know that there are 195 countries in the world? Each of them has a capital city. Some of them even have more than one capital and South Africa has three capitals! Some capitals aren't difficult to learn. For example, it's easy to remember that Mexico City is the capital of Mexico or that Brasilia is the capital of Brazil. We know the names of other capitals because we hear about them in History lessons, the news or sporting events.

You might know that the capital of Spain is Madrid and the capital of Greece is Athens. You may even know that the German capital is Berlin or that the Portuguese capital is Lisbon, but did you know that the Indian capital is New Delhi? Some capitals surprise us because they aren't the biggest city in the country. Did you know that the capital of Australia isn't Sydney? No, it's Canberra, and the capital of the USA isn't New York. It's Washington D.C.

1 What is the Mexican capital? Mexico City. _____

2 What is the capital of India? _____

3 Which country is Canberra the capital of? _____

4 What's the name of the Greek capital? _____

5 What is the Spanish capital? _____

6 What's the capital of Portugal? _____

7 Which country is Washington D.C. the capital of? _____

8 What is the Brazilian capital? _____

11 Complete the words with the groups of letters in the box. Use each group for only one pair of words.

sh	~~me~~	any	ey	co	al	try	ch	tal	th

1 Ro... _me_ ...tal   Yes (No)   **6** Portug... _____ ...ready   Yes No

2 Turk... _____ ...es   Yes No   **7** capi... _____ ...lest   Yes No

3 coun... _____ ...ing   Yes No   **8** Engli... _____ ...orts   Yes No

4 Germ... _____ ...where   Yes No   **9** nor... _____ ...rown   Yes No

5 Fren... _____ ...opsticks   Yes No   **10** Mexi... _____ ...mb   Yes No

12 Say the pairs of words in Activity 11. Do the letters sound the same in both words? Circle 'Yes' or 'No'.

> Rome ... metal

13 Ask and answer. Write your friend's answers.

1 Have you ever eaten Spanish food?   _____   What was it? _____

2 Have you ever eaten Mexican food?   _____   What was it? _____

3 Have you ever eaten Indian food?   _____   What was it? _____

4 Have you ever eaten Portuguese food?   _____   What was it? _____

5 Have you ever eaten Italian food?   _____   What was it? _____

6 Have you ever eaten Greek food?   _____   What was it? _____

7 Have you ever eaten _____ food?   _____   What was it? _____

8 Have you ever eaten _____ food?   _____   What was it? _____

14 Write a report about international food that you and your friend have eaten.

We haven't eaten Greek food, but I have eaten Portuguese food. I can't remember the word, but it was fish with tomatoes. It was delicious. Igor has eaten Mexican food. He had _____

_____

_____

_____

_____

_____

_____

_____

15 Complete the lists.

| foggy | ~~shorts~~ | keyboards | gold | biscuits | torches | science | went |

1 Shirts, skirts, trainers and _shorts_ .
2 Butter, jam, sauce, popcorn and _____ .
3 English, geography, art, maths and _____ .
4 Leather, metal, wool and _____ .
5 Lived, wanted, wished and _____ .
6 Sunny, cloudy, windy and _____ .
7 Laptops, webcams, headphones and _____ .
8 Tents, rucksacks, sleeping bags and _____ .

16 🎧11 CD4 Listen, check and say.

17 Write these words in order of size from the biggest to the smallest.

| city | continent | country | Earth | street | our solar system |
| town | ~~the universe~~ | village |

the universe _____

18 Read and complete Robert's form.

Woman: How can I help you?

Robert: I'd like to go on your Summer English Course in England.

Woman: Fine, now I need some information to put on the form. First, your name and surname, please.

Robert: Robert Schmidt.

Woman: OK, and when were you born?

Robert: On 15 June 1996.

Woman: Where are you from?

Robert: I'm from Germany.

Woman: And your address, please?

Robert: I live at 35 Bear Street, Berlin.

Woman: What's the postcode?

Robert: I think it's 10117.

Woman: Good, and finally what's your telephone number?

Robert: Err, 689-730241.

Completing a form
• Read the headings carefully.
• Does the form want you to use CAPITAL letters?
• Do you have to circle or tick anything?

Write it right

Please use CAPITAL letters.
Name: ROBERT _____
Surname: _____
Course (please circle): music / art / English / sport
Date of birth: _____
Country of birth: _____
Nationality: _____
Address: _____
Postcode: _____
Telephone number: _____

19 Read and answer.

1 What's Iyam just done? He's just pushed the corn symbol.

2 How long has the museum at Balankanche been open? _____

3 How did the Mayas water their fields? _____

4 How long have Interpol wanted Iyam and Richard Tricker? _____

5 What are Sir Doug Bones and Diggory going to do with the Sun Stone? _____

6 What did Emily's grandfather use to follow them? _____

20 Do the Mayan quiz. True (T) or False (F)?

1 The Aztecs built the modern day Mexico City on a lake called Texcoco because they saw a Quetzal bird there. T / **F**

2 The Mayas studied the Sun, the Moon and the stars to measure time. T / F

3 For the Aztecs, gold was the most important material in their lives. T / F

4 The Mayas used picture writing or 'glyphs' to communicate by writing. T / F

5 The Mayas played musical instruments. Some of these were made of turtle shells, wood and sea shells. T / F

6 The Pyramid of Kukulcan sounds like a Quetzal bird singing when someone climbs it. T / F

7 The Mayas played a ball game called Tlachtli. It's like a cross between modern volleyball and basketball. T / F

8 Aztec braves painted their faces and wore birds' feathers and animal fur to look beautiful and to make people love them. T / F

9 The first chewing gum was made from soft rubber from trees. The Mayas used it to clean their teeth. T / F

10 The form of a snake moves up and down the north stairs of the Pyramid of The Sun: up in March and down in September. T / F

Answers:
1 False. Because they saw an eagle there and thought it was a sign from their gods.
3 False. Quetzal feathers were more important than gold.
6 False. This happens when someone claps their hands.
8 False. They painted their faces and wore these things to look horrible and to make people feel afraid of them.

? Do you remember?

1 It's seven o'clock in the evening. Have you done your homework yet?_____

2 Yes, I've _____ finished it! I finished it ten seconds ago.

3 Paris is the _____ of France.

4 People in Mexico speak _____.

5 I have been to Germany, France and Spain but I can't speak _____, _____ or _____.

6 'What _____ are you?' 'I'm Portuguese.'

Can do   I can talk about what has already or just happened and what hasn't happened yet.

I can talk about different countries and nationalities.

I can complete a form in English.

1 Complete the text with words from the box.

| Chinese | started | ~~book~~ | people | Russia | important | years |

This **(1)** book_____ is in the Latin alphabet. The people of Rome in Italy **(2)** _____ using the
Latin alphabet more than 2,700 **(3)** _____ ago. Now more than
two billion **(4)** _____ use it.
There are also a lot of other **(5)** _____ alphabets. After the Latin alphabet, the next
most popular ways of writing are the Chinese script and the Devanagari alphabet from India. About
1.2 billion people use the **(6)** _____ script and 1 billion use the Devanagari alphabet. Then
there is the Arabic alphabet, which is used by half a billion (500 million) people, and the Cyrillic
alphabet. There are about 300 million people from Central and Eastern Europe, for example
in **(7)** _____ , who use the Cyrillic alphabet. There are a lot of other ways of writing too.

2 Read again and answer.

1 What alphabet are you using to answer this question? The Latin alphabet._____
2 How old is it? _____
3 How many people use it today? _____
4 What alphabet do Indian people use? _____
5 What is the name of the other alphabet from Central and Eastern Europe? _____
6 How many people write in it? _____

3 Where are these English words from? Label the map.

| kiwi | kangaroo | karate | ~~igloo~~ | opera | athlete | chocolate |

1 igloo_____

2 _____

3 _____

4 _____

5 _____

6 _____

7 _____

Greenland

Italy

Greece

Mexico

Japan

Australia

New Zealand

4 Think of a word from your language that you would like to give to English.
Write a letter to a dictionary writer saying why they should add this word
to the dictionary.

5 **Read the diary and write the missing words. Write one word on each line.**

Friday 4 April

Example   This evening I'm writing my diary ....in............ Paris!

1   Paris is the capital of .... I am here because I

2   want to learn to .... French better and to see the

3   city, of course. Today I .... to the Eiffel Tower

    with my friends. It's really tall and it looks very beautiful. I

4   .... some great photos.

5   Tomorrow we're .... to visit a famous museum

    which is called the Louvre so we can see the 'Mona Lisa'. I

    can't wait!

Review Units 7 and 8

1 Read the story. Choose a word from the box. Write the correct word next to numbers 1–5.

umbrellas | ~~just~~ | worn | Paris | belt | same | pockets | Spanish | capital | button

Friendly

Dan, Alvin and Shari are sad because the second series of *Friendly* has just____ ended. They all agree that the funniest episode of this series was 'Jim's new clothes'.

In this episode Jim and Peter went to London to buy some new clothes. They caught the train to the **(1)** _____ one Saturday morning. They found a shop called Fine Fashion. The salesman told them that all the clothes came from **(2)** _____ , the capital of France and the capital of fashion.

Jim bought some big, green trousers with **(3)** _____ above the knees. He bought a light grey T-shirt and a black **(4)** _____ . He liked his new clothes and he decided to wear them home.

When they went back to the station, they saw Jim's grandfather, but it was very funny because his grandpa's trousers were big and green with pockets above the knees. He was also wearing a light grey T-shirt and a black belt. His clothes were the **(5)** _____ as Jim's.

2 Now choose the best name for the story.

Tick one box. Streets ahead ☐   Capital cities ☐   The latest fashion ☐

3 Read and match the jokes.

1 What do you call an elephant at the North Pole?
2 What did the scarf say to the hat?
3 Why do birds fly south in winter?
4 What must we break before we can use it?
5 What kind of key opens a banana?
6 What do you get if you cross a kangaroo with an elephant?
7 What do you call an elephant with a carrot in each ear?
8 What do sea monsters eat?
9 How far can you walk into the wood?
10 What's the best thing to put into ice cream?

a Anything you want because it can't hear you!
b A monkey!
c A spoon!
d Lost!
e Because it's easier than walking!
f Half way. Then you're walking out of the wood.
g You go on ahead, I'll just hang around.
h Big holes in Australia!
i An egg.
j Fish and ships.

1

4 Complete the sentences. Count and write the letters.

1 <u>Shorts</u> are short trousers. We wear them in summer.

2 Hindi, French and Portuguese are different _____ .

3 We wear _____ on our hands.

4 A hundred years is a _____ .

5 He's just _____ his coat on. He's going out.

6 Africa is a _____ .

7 You might have a _____ inside your jacket. You can carry things in it.

8 The cities of London, Paris and Rome are all _____ .

9 We use this to close our shirts and coats. It can be different shapes and colours. _____

10 We wear a _____ at the top of our trousers or jeans so they don't fall down.

11 'What _____ is she?' 'She's Chinese.'

12 Oh, no! It's just started to rain and I've left my _____ at home!

13 We wear _____ on our feet, often to do sport.

14 Special clothes to protect us. A fire fighter wears one. _____

5 Now complete the crossword. Write the message.

s h o r t s

1	2	3	4	5	6		7	4	6	7
							h			h |!

6 Quiz time!

1 Why was Dan's shirt funny at the disco?
<u>It was</u> _____

2 How long have people in China worn Han clothes? _____

3 What were moccasins? _____

4 How many countries won the ezine competition? _____

5 Where is sushi from? _____

6 What does the prefix 'tele-' mean? _____

7 Write questions for your quiz in your notebook.

1 Write sentences with 'should' or 'shouldn't'.

1 be careful / chat / internet <u>You should be careful when you chat on the internet.</u>
2 spend / more than an hour a day / a computer screen _____
3 be afraid / use technology _____
4 play exciting computer games / before / bed _____
5 get angry / you can't use a computer _____

2 Read and answer.

David's older sister, Jenny, thinks he's got a problem with computers. He spends more than two hours a day in front of the screen and he's very unhappy when he hasn't got an internet connection. He spends all weekend at home playing on the computer and he doesn't want to go out with his friends. When his parents call him for family meals he takes about 10 minutes to go to the table.

Then he gets angry when he has to help the family to clean up after the meal. He only wants to go back to the computer. Last Sunday, Jenny saw him playing games on the computer at three o'clock in the morning when the family were all in bed.

1 Who thinks David's got a problem? <u>Jenny</u>
2 How much time does he spend on the computer every day? _____
3 Why doesn't he want to go out with his friends? _____
4 What was he doing at three o'clock in the morning last Sunday? _____
5 Do you think David's got a problem? _____
6 What do you think Jenny should do? _____
_____

Be safe at home

① Read and choose the answer.

How safe are you?

1 Your hands are dirty from playing in the garden. There are some biscuits on the kitchen table. What should you do?

a Clean your hands on your trousers and take a biscuit.
b Eat two biscuits quickly before your little sister comes.
c Wash your hands and then have a biscuit.

2 There's a heavy box of books on your bedroom floor. You have to take them to the car. What should you do?

a Put the books into two boxes and carry first one, then the other to the car.
b Pick up the box. It's difficult but you try to take it very quickly.
c Ask your little sister to carry the box for you.

3 You want to get a glass from the highest shelf in the cupboard. What should you do?

a Climb onto a chair and put your hands above your head to get it.
b Ask your mum or dad to help you.
c Pick up your little brother and put him on your shoulders so he can get it for you.

4 You've dropped a bowl of water on the kitchen floor. What should you do?

a Dry the floor carefully because it's dangerous to walk on.
b Go outside and play. Somebody else can clean it.
c Put a chair over the water so nobody can see it.

② Write a safety contract for your home.

1 _We must put our toys away safely._
2 _____
3 _____
4 _____
5 _____

_____ got the Safety at Home certificate.

Congratulations!

Safety at home

Harmony at home

1 Read and choose the right words.

Last month I went to a small **(1) countryside / city / village** in Africa and watched how families worked together. In these families, the children help their parents and **(2) everyone / everywhere / anyone** works. For example, if there are three children, the oldest looks **(3) under / at / after** the youngest when the parents are working. The other child stays with the family animals, like goats or sheep. Every day the two older **(4) parents / children / animals** get the water. They have **(5) got / to / at** walk two kilometres to get it. They haven't got a TV, a computer or a lot of **(6) free / the / good** time, but I found that they're **(7) happy / happier / happiest** than some children in different countries who have all these things.

2 Write about how you help at home. Use the pictures and questions to help you.

What jobs do you do at home?
What jobs do your mum, dad, brothers and sisters do?
Do you enjoy doing jobs at home? Why? Why not?
How do you feel when you help at home?

	At home, I do several things to help. I

1 Read and answer.

1 There's a new boy at school. How can you help him to make friends?

----

2 Some children at school have started calling you horrible names. What should you do?

----

3 Your little brother has a big problem at school. He's asked you not to tell anybody. You think the problem is serious. What are you going to do?

----

4 Your group of friends at school don't like a girl. They've told you not to go out with this girl or they won't talk to you. What should you do?

----

5 One of your friends has sent some horrible messages to another student at school. What are you going to do?

----

2 Talk about your ideas with your friend. Do you agree?

(I agree.) (I don't agree. I think …)

3 Read and match.

1 I'm very	**a** I do?		
2 They think	**b** angry.	1	
3 This isn't	**c** very worried.		
4 What should	**d** help me.		
5 I feel	**e** the first time.		
6 Please	**f** it's funny.		

4 Imagine you have a problem at home or school. Write a letter to Betty and Robert. Use phrases from Activity 3 to help you.

5 Swap letters with a friend. Read your friend's letter and give him / her some advice.

(You should / shouldn't …) (You have to …)

(The best idea is to …) (You must / mustn't …)

Grammar reference

⭐ **Complete the sentences.** | should | ~~Would~~ | Shall | Let's | mustn't | don't |

1 _Would_ _____ you like an ice cream?
2 You _____ play football in the road.
3 Why _____ we send her a text message?
4 _____ we chat online?
5 I _____ do my homework before I play on the computer.
6 _____ write an article for the ezine.

1 Write questions. Answer.

1 He / be an actor? (✗) _Is he going to be an actor?_ _No, he isn't._
2 They / see a film? (✓) _____
3 You / do your homework? (✓) _____
4 She / be in the play? (✗) _____
5 We / play tennis? (✗) _____
6 He / read a book about dragons? (✓) _____

2 Read and write.

1 They'll go to the Moon by plane. (rocket) _No, they won't. They'll go there by rocket._
2 She'll eat fruit. (special food) _____
3 I'll wear jeans. (skirt) _____
4 They'll fly to Jupiter. (Mars) _____
5 We'll leave next week. (next month) _____
6 There'll be a lot of people. (robots) _____

3 Read and match.

1	I was snowboarding		a	felt a mouse in his sleeping bag.	
2	They were waiting at the bus		b	forest when I dropped my torch.	
3	She was making bread		c	when she lost her ring.	
4	We were having a picnic when		d	when I fell and hurt my elbow.	1
5	I was walking through the		e	the storm began.	
6	He was sleeping when he		f	stop when they saw their friend.	

4 Read and circle the answer.

1 There are too **(many)** / **any** knives.
2 There **isn't** / **aren't** enough chairs.
3 She hasn't got **much** / **many** sugar.

4 They haven't got **too** / **enough** forks.
5 Did they have **much** / **many** sweets?
6 How **many** / **much** pasta do you want?

5 Complete the sentences. Write *for* or *since*.

1 She's had her computer <u>since</u> 2011.
2 We've studied English _____ five years.
3 I haven't played tennis _____ two weeks.
4 They've lived here _____ they were six.
5 He's been at his new school _____ three months.
6 She hasn't seen Peter _____ the summer.

6 Complete the sentences.

> somewhere   no-one   anything   something   ~~Everything~~   any

1 It's raining. <u>Everything</u> in the garden is wet.
2 I saw _____ interesting on TV last night.
3 The house was empty because _____ was at home.
4 He didn't have _____ money so he didn't go to the cinema.
5 I want to go _____ exciting on holiday this year.
6 Our town is really boring for young people. There isn't _____ to do.

7 Read and order the words.

1 (go to) (this evening) (We might) (the cinema)

<u>We might go to the cinema this evening.</u>

2 (I'm tired) (leave the disco) (I may) (early because)

_____

3 (They may not) (their project) (have time) (to finish)

_____

8 Write the sentences in the present perfect. Use the words given.

1 (just) I arrive at the airport.   <u>I've just arrived at the airport.</u>
2 (yet) He not be to New York.   _____
3 (already) I tidy my room.   _____
4 (yet) you write that email?   _____
5 (just) He wake up.   _____
6 (already) They finish the book.   _____

Irregular verbs

Infinitive	Past tense	Past participle
be	was / were	been
be called	was / were called	been called
be going to	was / were going to	been going to
begin	began	begun
break	broke	broken
bring	brought	brought
buy	bought	bought
can	could	–
catch	caught	caught
choose	chose	chosen
come	came	come
cut	cut	cut
do	did	done
draw	drew	drawn
drink	drank	drunk
drive	drove	driven
dry	dried	dried
eat	ate	eaten
fall	fell	fallen
fall over	fell over	fallen over
feel	felt	felt
find	found	found
find out	found out	found out
fly	flew	flown
forget	forgot	forgotten
get	got	got
get (un)dressed	got (un)dressed	got (un)dressed
get (up / on / off)	got (up / on / off)	got (up / on / off)
get to	got to	got to
give	gave	given
go	went	gone / been
go out	went out	gone / been out
go shopping	went shopping	gone / been shopping
grow	grew	grown
have	had	had
have got	had	had
have (got) to	had to	had to
hear	heard	heard
hide	hid	hidden
hit	hit	hit
hold	held	held
hurt	hurt	hurt
keep	kept	kept
know	knew	known

Infinitive	Past tense	Past participle
learn	learnt / learned	learnt / learned
leave	left	left
let	let	let
lie down	lay down	lain down
lose	lost	lost
make	made	made
make sure	made sure	made sure
mean	meant	meant
meet	met	met
must	had to	had to
put	put	put
put on	put on	put on
read	read	read
ride	rode	ridden
run	ran	run
say	said	said
see	saw	seen
sell	sold	sold
send	sent	sent
should	–	–
sing	sang	sung
sit	sat	sat
sleep	slept	slept
smell	smelt / smelled	smelt / smelled
speak	spoke	spoken
spell	spelt / spelled	spelt / spelled
spend	spent	spent
stand	stood	stood
steal	stole	stolen
swim	swam	swum
swing	swung	swung
take	took	taken
take a photo / picture	took a photo / picture	taken a photo / picture
take off	took off	taken off
teach	taught	taught
tell	told	told
think	thought	thought
throw	threw	thrown
understand	understood	understood
wake up	woke up	woken up
wear	wore	worn
win	won	won
write	wrote	written